INTERIOR PAINT FINISHES AND EFFECTS

STEWART MCDONALD

INTERIOR PAINT FINISHES AND EFFECTS

THE CROWOOD PRESS

CONTENTS

INTRODUCTION

My goal in writing this book is to share an extensive range of paint finishes for all. I plan to showcase not only traditional, but also contemporary methods and applications, which will aid the modern craftsperson. Owing to the overwhelming scope and number of paint finishes possible, I have limited this book to those which I hope the reader will find most practical and functional. It is my hope that as wide a range of people as possible can use this book, from the trade decorator to the beginner, and all can hopefully gain a wealth of skills from it.

For centuries, humans have used painted finishes to adorn walls from the humblest of homes to the grandest of palaces, from the most basic revamp of a living room table or cabinet, to the Marbling of columns in the most opulent interiors imaginable.

What exactly is a painted finish? It is a paint or pigment which is mixed with a transparent medium to give a semi-translucent coating called a glaze. This is then applied to a dry undercoat and manipulated with an array of tools and materials whilst wet. Overlaying these coloured glazes (sometimes many times) has allowed the craftsperson to create the most beautiful surfaces, from rare and exotic woods and marbles to the most breathtaking Trompe l'Oeil murals. The finish itself comes under many names including: faux, paint effect, broken colour, scumbling, glazing and decorative painting. From these, three main finishes have emerged: Graining, Marbling and Trompe l'Oeil. Graining is the imitation of wood, Marbling the imitation of marble, and Trompe l'Oeil, the painting of light and shadow on a surface to create the illusion of depth and structure. As a practising decorative artist and teacher, I will cover all of these in depth, providing a workable how-to guide on producing all kinds of paint effects, from the simplest for beginners, to faux art masterpieces for the seasoned professional.

Although some of the higher end finishes included in this book may be beyond the average painter, I hope that they can use the examples and illustrations here as friendly 'ambition' for what can be achieved with dedication and practice.

I have structured this book in a way that I hope will benefit the reader most effectively. Firstly, the tools and materials required to produce all the finishes in this book are discussed. This is followed by information on all the paints and glazes needed, then subsequent chapters on producing the actual finishes. Throughout the book there are photographs and examples of my own work as reference and, hopefully, inspiration. Finally, I hope that whoever uses this book will have learned something new.

2"
2"

GETTING STARTED

Before applying your painted finish, serious consideration must be given to a number of factors, the most important of which is health and safety. When using paints of any kind, good ventilation must be provided. All floor areas must be covered with good-quality dust sheets, and fragile items such as paintings, furniture, and so on, removed, or covered with polythene sheeting. Wet paint signs should be put up in the area that is being painted, and prearranged cleaning facilities must be used. A professional clean, tidy and friendly manner should be adopted at all times, with the work area cleared and tidied at the end of the working day.

The single most important health and safety issue for the painter is the disposal of rags. When working in oils, because of the linseed oil content, discarded rags can sometimes spontaneously combust. All rags should be put in a bucket of water immediately after use, and all rags disposed of at the end of the week at your local refuse centre.

Liaising with the customer is also very important. Good, clear ongoing dialogue and communication is crucial during the course of a job, with a clear timescale of how long the job will take and what, if any, disruption is likely to occur. Details of the painter's public and product liability insurance should always be available to the customer also.

SAMPLE PANELS

Quite often, the painter will be asked to provide a sample panel of the paint finish being applied for the customer's inspection. More recently, with the advent of social media and images on mobile phones, this practice has now lessened somewhat. However, the painter should always be ready to provide some, if asked. For transportation purposes, I provide these on painted lining paper. I do generally provide these free of charge if the job quote has been accepted and agreed, but as they can be time-consuming, I charge a fee if it has not.

PREPARATION

Almost as important as the paint finish itself is surface preparation. The old saying 'fail to prepare, prepare to fail' has never been truer when applied to painting. So, what exactly is preparation? For our purposes, we can break it down into three stages:

1. Sanding down
2. Priming
3. Base coating.

Sanding down

This generally takes place on previously painted surfaces. Nowadays, I almost always use an electric sander with dust extraction. This gives the quickest and best sanded surface, with zero dust. Of course, hand sanding can always be substituted. Depending on the roughness of the surface, I almost always use 80 grit sandpaper. This is robust enough to take care of really rough surfaces, but not so coarse as to leave scratch marks that will be visible when painted over.

Priming

The single most important part of preparation is priming. Using a compatible primer that adheres to the surface properly is absolutely crucial. If the primer isn't correct, what goes on afterwards is futile, and the painter is facing unmitigated disaster. Imagine preparing, painting and executing a fantastic finish, only to find it scratches easily or comes off with even the slightest abrasion. This makes choosing the proper primer essential. As a failsafe, I use Zinsser B-I-N primer whenever I'm priming. It is shellac based, quick drying and adheres to almost all surfaces exceptionally. A single coat of primer only is required.

Base coating

In almost all cases, paint finishes are carried out on either an eggshell or satin basecoat. Gloss surfaces are too shiny, which makes the glaze slide about and hard to manipulate. It also lessens the adhesion between the two coatings, giving the possibility of flaking occurring when dry. Matt finishes are too flat, which means the glaze tends to sink into the surface, making it hard to manipulate. Either water- or oil-based coatings can be used. It is important to give two coats of basecoat. Even if a single basecoat may look good and has visually covered well, the surface may still be slightly rough in places, resulting in unsightly patches occurring when the glaze is applied.

Finish or topcoat

A finish or topcoat seals and protects your work. These usually come in the form of varnishes, either water based or oil based. For speed, I usually use water-based varnishes to finish my work. These allow me to apply two coats in quick succession and finish the job promptly. Care must be taken, however, if using what are called water-based 'floor varnishes'. These include much harsher solvents, and can irreparably damage the painted finish.

Oil-based varnishes can, of course, be used, and indeed can arguably give a smoother overall finish. However, they do tend to yellow slightly over time, and for this reason are unsuitable for some of the lighter, whiter finishes such as Carrara Marbling, for example. I do sometimes prefer to use an oil-based varnish over my Graining work, as the slight yellowing can actually enhance and enrich the finish over time.

Oil on top of water, and water on top of oil

A lot of the finishes in this book call for a combination of both water- and oil-based coatings. As a rule, any oil-based coating can be applied over a water-based one comfortably. When applying water over oil, however, care must be taken, as the water-based coating won't properly adhere to the oil-based one. To resolve this, it is always best to 'degrease' the oil-based surface with a fuller's earth solution. This is done by simply mixing some fuller's earth powder into a little water, mixing it, then sponging the surface to be painted thoroughly. This should comprehensively degrease the surface, making it suitable to receive a water-based coating.

MATERIALS

The tools and equipment needed to carry out paint finishes can sometimes be quite extensive. For this reason, I have separated this chapter into three parts:

1. Glazes: the mediums required to carry out the finishes, and how to mix them.
2. Brushes: a list of all the brushes required.
3. Tools: all the tools needed for manipulating the glaze.

Glazes and scumbles

Almost all decorative paint finishes are carried out using a glaze or scumble. These coatings are the single most important component in decorative painting. When mixing a glaze, they are made up of three components:

1. A solid paint medium, which usually comes in the form of artist's oils or acrylics.
2. A clear glaze, which is a transparent thick liquid.
3. A thinner, which is either white spirit for oil, or water for acrylic. When mixed, this gives the desired coloured glaze or scumble.

Acrylic glaze is best bought from a supplier and is mostly called acrylic glaze or scumble.

Oil-based glaze/scumble can similarly be bought, but it is relatively easy (and a lot cheaper) to make and mix yourself.

To make your own, the ratios are: 3 parts boiled linseed oil; 1 part terebine driers; 0.5 part water. To make it, take an empty container and add the linseed oil. Add half the driers, close and shake vigorously. Add the other half and shake. Finally, add the water and shake. The water acts as a lightening agent and prevents the scumble from becoming too dark.

Brushes

As well as the conventional paintbrush everyone is familiar with, there is an extensive range of brushes, which have been developed over the years for the decorative painter. Choosing the correct brush is crucial to the finish sought. The most important brush required is the badger softener. This brush is used to blend and soften media, particularly in Marbling, Graining and Trompe l'Oeil. Investing in a good badger softener is invaluable and, with proper care, will last a lifetime.

THE MOST COMMONLY USED BRUSHES

- badger softener
- dragging brush
- flogger
- mottler
- fan overgrainer
- fan fitch
- thin overgrainer
- flat fitch
- Chinese calligraphy brush
- 1-inch paintbrush
- trimmed flat fitch
- long rigger brush

Tools

When it comes to the tools required for paint finishes, on one hand, the sheer number can seem quite daunting; on the other, most of the tools cost next to nothing and can be acquired or manufactured by the painter quite easily from readily available materials. For one finish in particular, Graining, the number of tools and brushes developed over the years is vast. However, I have tried to limit and simplify the number here, and have only listed the tools which are required to carry out the finishes in this book.

Materials

1. Low quality brushes (splayed)
2. Flat decorator's paint tray
3. Acrylic scumble
4. Oil-based scumble
5. Swan feathers
6. Crackle glaze
7. Sea sponge
8. White spirit
9. 120 grit straight edges
10. 2-inch paint brush
11. Kolner gold leaf system and gold leaf
12. Chinese calligraphy brushes
13. Hog's hair stippler
14. Artists' oil paints
15. Hog's hair fan overgrainer
16. Badger softener
17. Fan fitches
18. Precision edge masking and lining tape
19. Make up blending brushes
20. English Oak sketch book
21. Maroger oil medium
22. Fine lining and rigger brushes
23. Artists' acrylic paints
24. Hog's hair graining mottlers
25. Veining horns
26. Neatsfoot oil
27. Hessian cloth
28. Chamois leather and cotton rag
29. Metal graining combs
30. Rubber graining combs
31. Rattan matt
32. Cork graining combs

SETTING UP

Paints, oils and palettes

How you set up to carry out any project is vitally important, from a small practice piece at home to a large commission or job of work. If I am doing a large job, say for example a Graining job, once everything is prepared, basecoated and ready to go, I'll commence setting up for the job. I first mix my base scumble in a pot, making enough to carry out the whole job. I test this before I start, getting the glaze and oil proportions correct, and to see how the actual finish looks.

I also always have a flat painter's tray by my side when I'm working, with a small squeeze of the oils I have used on the tray. I use this to add variations of shade and colour as I go.

This tray is crucial, and fundamental to my way of working.

It is the best, cleanest way of working when you are carrying out any job, big or small. I also use it exclusively when I'm doing exhibition work or smaller panels. It is ideally suited: I use the trough to hold the clear scumble, which is then used to mix with the oil or acrylic colours that are squeezed on to the flat surface of the tray. The tray keeps the paint and scumble mixes enclosed and secure. The tray can be covered with cling film or another inverted tray overnight to preserve the tube colours and scumble mixes and prevent them from drying. I paint the tray white, to help with colour mixing. All the panels in this book have been painted using this method. Flat artist's palettes should never be used. In almost all areas of decorative painting, we are working with semi-fluid media, and because of this, palettes are messy, sloppy and extremely unsuitable. Working cleanly is the first and most important rule of decorative painting.

GLAZE/PAINT MIX RATIO

One of the most common mistakes people make in decorative painting is the paint/glaze mix ratio when mixing a scumble for a project. The problem is that the ratio varies a great deal between subjects and applications, and is a matter of practice and familiarity. But a good rule of thumb is that the amount of artist's oil or acrylic in the scumble is much, much smaller than one would imagine.

Below is a rough guideline ratio only, to give the reader an indicator of the quantities required.

- Artists oil/acrylic: 1.25
- Clear glaze or scumble: 40ml

PART ONE
PAINT EFFECTS

In the world of decorative painting, mastering the art of high-end paint finishes is a journey that begins with the fundamental techniques of broken colour work. These techniques lay the foundation for more elaborate finishes such as Marbling, Graining and Trompe l'Oeil, which are explored in depth in later chapters.

Marbling, with its intricate patterns and textures, is achieved through techniques such as Rag Rolling, which are essential skills to acquire. While one may not need to master all the techniques featured in this chapter to excel in a specific finish such as Graining, understanding colour mixing, glaze application and proportions is invaluable for any aspiring decorative painter or hobbyist.

Within this chapter, seven finishes are highlighted, each offering a unique opportunity for you to achieve these finishes, and the techniques provide a diverse range of faux painting styles for you to explore and perfect.

For beginners, it is crucial to follow the prescribed rules diligently, allowing for repetitive practice until the techniques become second nature, like a personal signature. By mastering the basics, you can then begin to modify and evolve these techniques, tailoring them to your individual style and preferences.

Craquelure and Gilding, while not techniques themselves, offer distinct applications that can elevate any painting project. These relatively simple yet impactful finishes add a touch of sophistication and elegance to various surfaces, making them valuable skills for painters to possess.

In conclusion, mastering high-end paint finishes requires dedication, practice and a willingness to explore new techniques. By starting with the basics and gradually progressing to more advanced finishes, painters can expand their skill set and unlock endless creative possibilities in the world of decorative painting.

The seven finishes in this chapter are: Rag Rolling, Faux Stone, Antiquing, Dragging, Tortoiseshell, Craquelure and Gilding.

I have chosen these to give as wide a range of faux painting techniques as possible for the painter to learn and master. For the beginner, it is important to learn these techniques, and to follow certain rules rigidly and faithfully for their reproduction. Repetition is the key, until it becomes second nature, like your own signature. Then, once mastered, they can be modified and progressed to your own capacity and taste.

As explained previously, Craquelure and Gilding aren't techniques as such, but more applications. I have included them here as they are relatively simple to learn, but give a unique, striking finish wherever utilised and are always a great skill to have in any painter's arsenal.

Upcycled Louis VX style furniture, featuring Craquelure (*see* page 36) Antiquing (*see* page 24) and Gilding (*see* page 42).

RAG ROLLING

The Foundation of Decorative Painting

Rag Rolling stands as an indispensable technique within the canon of decorative painting. It is revered as *the* quintessential paint effect that serves as a cornerstone for a myriad of decorative paint finishes. Widely embraced and celebrated for its versatility, this broken colour technique holds universal acclaim as a fundamental starting point for decorative paint finishes.

Rag Rolling effortlessly gives a touch of elegance and depth to a variety of surfaces such as walls, furniture, picture frames and mouldings, enhancing them with its broken colour and unique variation.

Its simplicity belies its transformative power, making it not just the simplest, but also one of the most visually striking finishes in a decorative painter's repertoire.

To embark on a journey into the world of decorative painting without first mastering Rag Rolling would be akin to building a house without a solid foundation. It is a skill that lays the groundwork for more advanced effects, serving as a gateway to the decorative painting goals that lie beyond. The skills acquired through the practice of Rag Rolling, whether in colour harmony, glaze application or the manipulation of light and shadow, form the bedrock of a decorative painter's toolkit. It is essential for creating captivating and visually engaging finishes; finishes which are the building blocks upon which more complex decorative effects are constructed.

It is the simplest, quickest and most transformative of all the decorative painting effects. But it is not just something to be learned as a stepping stone into decorative painting: it is a time-honoured and classic finish within itself.

However, Rag Rolling *does* serve as a gateway to mastering Marbling and other broken colour finishes; finishes that absolutely use the skills honed through mastering Rag Rolling. As we delve deeper into the art of decorative painting in this book, we will come to appreciate the foundational role that Rag Rolling plays in shaping our journey through the decorative arts, and guiding us towards an understanding and mastering of broken colour and professional paint finishes.

Step-by-step

RAG ROLLING

Black and gold is a classic colour combination. I have executed this on a yellow ochre sunburst ground, achieved by coating the centre of a white eggshell base with yellow ochre artist's acrylic. I then stippled out from the centre with a hog hair stippler. When this was dry, I taped it in an art nouveau design. The tape was then given a thinned coating of water-based matt varnish and allowed to dry. This prevents paint bleed-through, and gives perfect, clean lines when removed.

MATERIALS

- oil scumble
- black artist's oil paint
- hog hair stippler
- chamois leather

Coat the entire panel with an oil glaze mix of pure black.

With a hog hair stippler, remove all brush marks by giving the panel a light, even stipple.

Slightly dampen a leather chamois, then scrunch it up and begin to roll the surface. After every pass, shake out the rag and scrunch again. This prevents pattern repetition and paint build up.

Scrunch the rag to a point between your fingers and press down on any gaps in the pattern. This helps give a uniform pattern.

Repeat this technique, opening the rag out periodically to prevent repetition, as above.

To finish, remove the tape.

FAUX STONEWORK

Historically called stone blocking, faux stone or brickwork has been one of the most utilised techniques in the architectural and decorative arts. Stones possessing high strength such as sandstone and granite, along with marble, were traditionally used both in block form for wall construction and for flooring. The imitation of these stones has a long history, with sandstone giving a much more subtle and understated finish than its marble cousins. Faux stone requires a very basic application of broken colour techniques, including spattering and bagging, to quickly and authentically replicate the diverse textures of individual blocks and slabs. The application of a Trompe l'Oeil effect I have included here isn't paramount in simulating the stone, but can enhance the final appearance, thereby giving the brickwork some depth. Giving the surface a three-dimensional look is aesthetically pleasing, but it isn't critical to the finish.

Creating high-quality brickwork requires exceptionally accurate sizing, layout and meticulous attention to planning detail. This level of precision is critical to ensuring that each segment aligns perfectly, mimicking the structure of authentic brickwork. This consideration is imperative to ensure the final look meets the desired visual and structural standards. The quality of the look is further enhanced by thoughtful consideration to the shade variation that plays a crucial part in imitating the natural differences found in real stone. This nuanced study will ensure an authentic and visually appealing finish, effectively replicating the appearance of genuine sandstone brickwork.

The finished piece.

MATERIALS

- 5mm (¼in) lining tape
- acrylic glaze
- artist's acrylic paint
  - yellow ochre
  - white
  - burnt umber
  - black
- newspaper
- badger softener
- splayed paintbrush

FAUX STONEWORK

On a light cream eggshell/satin surface, plan and tape your brickwork design and apply 5mm (¼in) lining tape to form the sandstone. Apply a thinned coat of matt acrylic varnish over the tape, and dry. This prevents bleed-through, and gives crisp, perfect lines when removed.

With an acrylic glaze mix of predominantly yellow ochre and a touch of burnt umber and a tiny bit of black, coat the entire surface.

Whilst wet, press a newspaper sheet flat onto the surface, press and rub with your palm, then remove and repeat.

Roll the newspaper and press the bag onto the surface lightly. Gently bag the entire surface. Allow to dry.

With the same glaze mix, coat individual bricks to slightly darken and create shade variation in the bricks. You can also add a touch of black or burnt umber for further variation on some. Repeat and mix.

Soften as you go with a badger softener.

Mix an acrylic colour of burnt umber, yellow ochre and white. Thin considerably with water *only*. With a stubby, cut-down synthetic brush, dab it in the paint mix, shake and flick off excess, and proceed to flick a fine mist spray onto the entire surface. This simulates the minute sand specks that are characteristic of sandstone. These can be blotted with newspaper if desired.

To finish, remove the tape. I have given the brickwork a slight 'trompe' shadow to the bottom and sides, but this is not necessary.

ANTIQUING

Antiquing is an enhancement technique based on two distinct approaches. The first method involves the intentional distressing and ageing of an object, usually furniture, to give it a rich, antique patina, while the second method focuses on highlighting and accentuating the existing decorative elements of ornate architectural fixtures, such as cornicing and decorative plasterwork.

These techniques can be employed individually or combined with a French Craqueleur effect (*see* page 36) for a transformative finish. They are used extensively to revamp and breathe new life into old and tired items of furniture. It can transform elaborate mouldings, cornices and centre roses into striking focal points that give a look of historic elegance. When applied to specific pieces of ornamentation, it enhances and brings to life the detail of that object.

The actual process of antiquing entails the application of glazes, wiping and distressing. When applied to furniture, it breathes new life into plain or dated pieces, imparting them with a distinctive, aged feel. By layering different amounts of glaze and selectively distressing specific areas, a beautiful finish resembling the natural patina of aged wood can be achieved. This technique is particularly beloved for the ability to create shabby chic or French farmhouse-style furniture, lending a sense of history and character to any item. Beyond furniture, antiquing can also enhance the look of mouldings, dados and wainscot panelling.

Cornices and centre roses, which are often found in traditional historic homes, can be transformed with this technique. By carefully applying glaze and strategically wiping certain areas, you can accentuate the beauty and detail of these architectural elements and create a sense of vintage grandeur.

When antiquing, it is as important to consider the overall style and colour scheme of the space to ensure a cohesive look. Experimenting with different techniques, colours or levels of distressing can help you achieve the desired effect and a truly unique and personalised finish.

Antiquing is a versatile painting technique that can be used to add warmth, character and a touch of nostalgia to a variety of surfaces. Whether you're looking to revitalise old furniture or enhance the architectural details of your home, antiquing is a wonderful way to infuse your space with a sense of history and style.

The finished piece.

ANTIQUING

The base surface for antiquing must be sealed with an eggshell or satin paint. This prevents the glaze from sinking into the surface and blotting, and ensures a clean wipe.

With an oil glaze of lamp black, coat the whole surface, ensuring all crevices are coated fully.

MATERIALS

- artist's oil paint
  - lamp black
- hog hair stippler
- cotton rag
- badger softener

With a hog hair stippler, stipple the entire surface to remove all brush marks.

Fold a pure cotton rag, about 30cm (12in) square, four times to create a perfectly smooth, flat pad that fits comfortably into your palm. Carefully and softly, begin wiping the very top of the surface, keeping the rag as flat as possible in your palm. The glaze should wipe off the high spots only, leaving residue in the crevices. Repeat, gradually applying more pressure as you go. To prevent your pad getting saturated with glaze, periodically unfold and refold it to a clean part as you go, ensuring a clean wipe.

Soften all with a badger softener. This will not only soften, but also slightly redistribute a very thin, almost indiscernible coating of glaze back onto all surfaces.

Finally, wipe again, targeting specific areas of interest and decorative value.

TORTOISESHELL

Tortoiseshell is traditionally derived from the hard shells of certain sea turtle species, most notably the hawksbill sea turtle. With its distinctive mottled patterns of amber yellows, blacks and browns, tortoiseshell has been prized for centuries for the creation of exquisite items including combs, jewellery, picture frames and also ornamental inlay items and even cabinetmaking.

However, today, the exploitation of tortoiseshell has given rise to significant conservation concerns, particularly regarding the critical endangerment of hawksbill sea turtles. Decorative artists are at the forefront in exploring ethical alternatives that mimic the visual qualities of tortoiseshell without posing a threat to the endangered turtle species. These endeavours represent a crucial step towards addressing the ecological implications of tortoiseshell endangerment. The process of creating faux tortoiseshell requires a medium to low level of skill. The decorative artist must overall possess an understanding of colour-blending techniques and the subtle use of the badger softener to replicate the distinctive variegated cloud-like patterning. I have rendered this tortoiseshell on imitation gold leaf, which gives an appealing golden lustre that shines through the finish; however, alternatively a bright yellow or scarlet red painted base is traditionally used.

The finished piece (close up).

Step-by-step

TORTOISESHELL

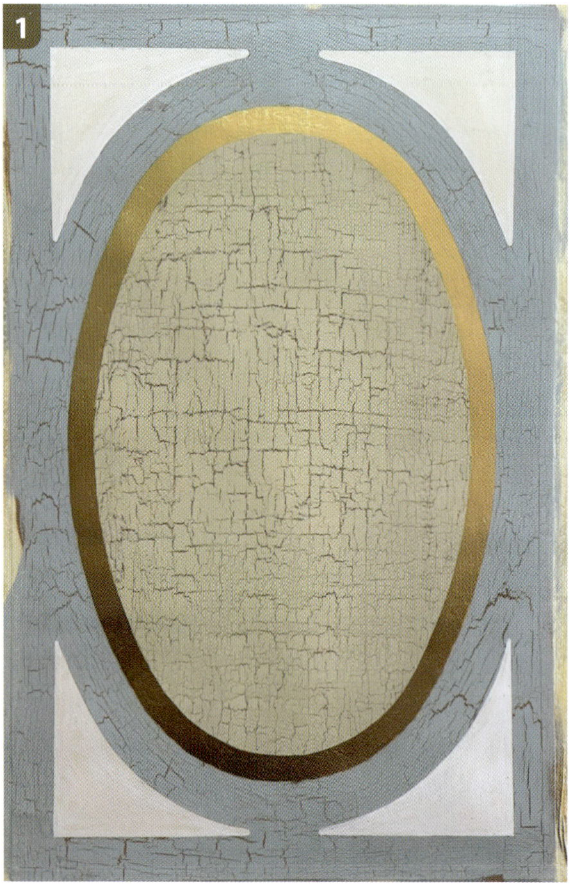

On a prepared surface, apply some imitation gold leaf.

Mix an oil scumble, dip a short, cut-down brush and spatter onto the surface.

MATERIALS

- gold leaf
- oil scumble
- artist's oil paint
  - burnt umber
- white spirit
- splayed paintbrush
- fan brush
- cotton rag
- badger softener

With the same brush, dab the scumble onto the surface. Vary the angle of the brush to avoid repetition.

Dip a coarse fan brush into white spirit. Shake off the excess, flick a fine mist onto the surface and ciss the surface.

Blot with a rag, and dab the surface, breaking up the glaze.

Finally, soften with a badger softening brush.

DRAGGING (OR STRIÉ)

Dragging is a basic decorative painting technique achieved by the manipulation of wet glaze on a surface by a particular tool in a straight line, creating a straight, linear pattern. A dry brush is used to create gentle vertical stripes with subtle variations in colour value, by meticulously dragging the brush vertically through the wet glaze, either freehand or with the aid of a straight edge. Various tools can be used to create dragging effects including traditional graining tools such as steel and rubber combs, and horsehair floggers. These tools can produce different textures and patterns, allowing painters to achieve a wide range of decorative effects. I have applied the effect twice here at right angles, with the help of a straight edge, to give a striking plaid effect. Dragging techniques can be applied to different surfaces in various ways, by crafting intricate borders on inlay projects, or embellishing architectural elements such as door panels, mouldings or skirtings. It is often used to great effect over gold leaf on picture frames and also japanned boxes and ornaments.

Once mastered, dragging can be used on doors and architraves to produce a very effective and fast woodgrain effect. This is known in the trade as brush graining, and is the gateway paint effect to oak graining. A simple dragging exercise using oak scumble with a few wiped highlights with a rag and thumbpiece can give a very convincing quartered oak reproduction. Once mastered, it can also be used to great effect in oak over-graining, to give the characteristic vertical Strié effect often found on quartered oak woodgraining.

The finished piece.

DRAGGING (OR STRIÉ)

On a white surface, design and draw your plan. Dragging can be done freehand, but as this exercise is all on a flat surface, I have made a straight edge to help. I attached 120 grit sandpaper on the bottom with double-sided tape. This allows the tool to be placed on wet glaze without disturbing the surface.

Mix an acrylic scumble to your desired colour and apply. Place your straight edge on the surface, and with a 2-inch synthetic cut-down brush, press firmly and run it down the surface, using the straight edge as a guide.

MATERIALS

- straight edge
- acrylic scumble
- artist's acrylic paint
  - yellow ochre
  - burnt umber
- 2-inch paintbrush: trimmed or cut down

Repeat on all surfaces, changing direction if desired.

Cross some areas at right angles, to achieve a linen effect.

I have finished this exercise with a red tortoiseshell inlay.

CRAQUELURE

Craquelure is a specific technique used in decorative painting that involves the deliberate introduction of fine cracks or fissures on the surface of an object to emulate an aged or antique appearance.

The process generally entails the application of two layers of coatings, one a dark basecoat and the top a lighter crackle glaze paint medium, which immediately cracks, giving a weathered or distressed effect. This can be applied to a wide array of surfaces including wood, metal, picture frames and even furniture to give a classic French Provençal distressed look.

A range of colour contrasts can be used, but I have used the classic dark basecoat with a cream and duck egg topcoat in an inlay setting. Some decorative artists resort to using their own specialised mediums or glazes, but I have found them to be unreliable, and because of this, commercially purchased mediums are by far the best method. The cracks can be regulated and manipulated when applied to give a variety of crack size and configuration. However, the process itself is very random, spontaneous and fast, and a few test pieces should always be carried out first. Craquelure is a striking, bold technique that can be used to enhance the visual appeal of otherwise plain decorative objects and furniture by giving them a timeworn, rich antique look.

▶ Craquelure is achieved by quickly applying a light-coloured crackle glaze onto a darker background, where the topcoat immediately begins to crack, revealing the darker ground. Test pieces should always be attempted first, as the crackle reaction can be very unpredictable.

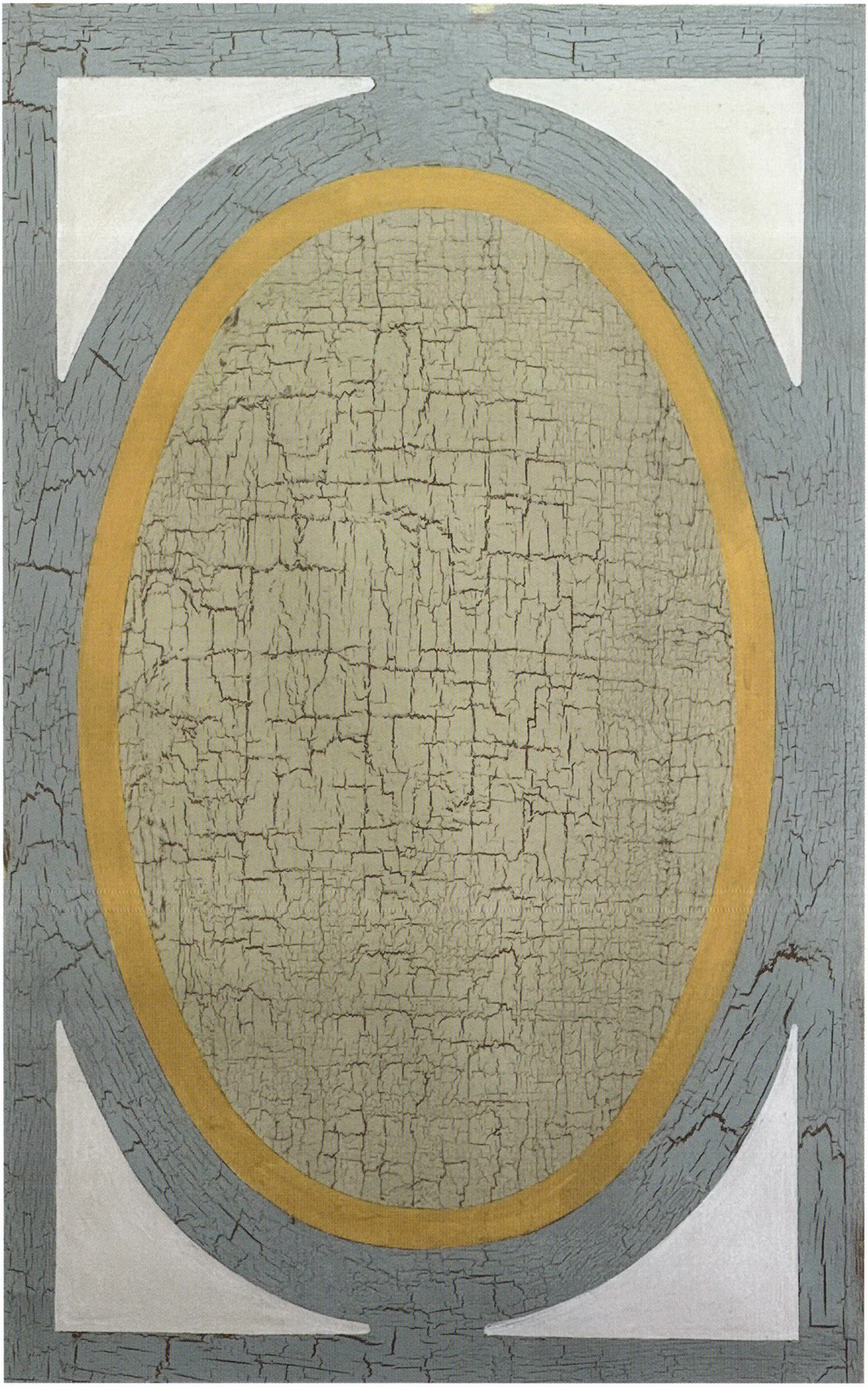

Step-by-step

CRAQUELURE

Apply a dark brown acrylic eggshell base onto a prepared surface. Allow to dry. Apply a coat of clear crackle glaze and allow to dry.

The cracking effect of craquelure can be controlled to a certain extent, with a bit of planning. A thin coat of the topcoat paint will produce thin cracks, and a thick coat will give thicker ones. I coated the panel thinner on the outside to complement the elliptical shape of the panel, giving thicker cracks in the middle, and thinner on the outside. You must be very quick at this stage. Apply a coat of cream acrylic eggshell paint to the surface.

MATERIALS

- crackle glaze
- hog hair overgrainer
- 2-inch paintbrush

With a hog hair overgrainer, manipulate the cracks as they start to appear, pushing and pulling them to produce larger cracks in the middle.

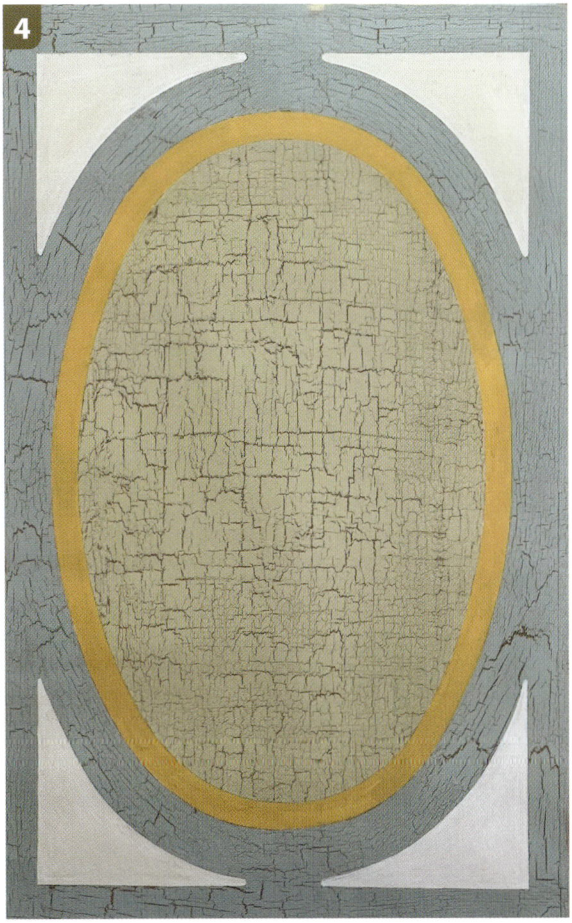

Repeat on the outside, with a different complementary colour, if desired. This craquelure finish forms the initial technique of the elaborate inlay panel featured later in this book (*see* page 120).`

GILDING

Gold leaf gilding (commonly known as just 'gilding') is an ancient craft that has been practised for thousands of years. The process of applying gold leaf to surfaces requires skill and precision that achieves a beautiful and durable finish which can last hundreds and, in some cases, even thousands of years. In the past, traditional Gilding was surrounded by mystique and complexity, but recent innovations have reinvented and simplified the process.

Summarised below are the essential elements and practices of traditional Gilding, as well as the key elements of the new, user-friendly process that I have showcased in this step-by-step workshop.

TRADITIONAL GILDING

Materials

Gold leaf is obtained by hammering out (usually by hand) small nuggets of solid gold, to infinitesimally small thin leaves, 250,000th of an inch thick, and 3¼ inches square. The leaves, loose or transfer, are placed in books of usually 25 leaves to each book. The leaf is available in various carats, with 22 carat gold leaf being the most used, due to its balance of purity and durability. The higher the carat, the purer the gold content in the leaf.

Application

Gold leaf is applied to a surface that has been coated with a special adhesive known as a 'size'. The size acts as a glue that adheres gold leaf to the surface. This surface is usually prepared and smoothed before the application of the gold leaf.

Types of gold leaf

There are two main forms of gold leaf used in Gilding: transfer leaf and loose leaf. Transfer leaf is attached to a thin sheet of tissue paper, making it easier to handle and manipulate. Loose leaf on the other hand comes in a free, unattached form and is typically manipulated and cut on a gilder's cushion before application.

Usage

Transfer leaf is often preferred for exterior work where handling and environmental factors come into play. Loose leaf, historically favoured for interior work, provides a superior finish, shine and lustre compared to transfer leaf. Water gilding produces the highest shine, the loose leaf being applied to a smoothed gesso surface using a water/gelatine mix, then burnished to a mirror finish when dry, using agate burnishers.

Techniques

Gilders use specialised tools such as brushes, knives and a gilder's tip (a tool for picking up and handling gold leaf) to apply and manipulate the gold leaf during the Gilding process.

Finishing

Once the gold leaf is applied, gilders may use techniques such as burnishing (rubbing the gold leaf to enhance its shine) and antiquing (applying a patina to give the gold an aged look) to achieve the desired effect.

NEW INNOVATIONS

In the world of Gilding, the big question has always been: can I get the bright, high-gloss look of loose-leaf water gilding with the easier-to-use transfer leaf? The answer has always been no. Oil gilding cannot be burnished and can never achieve the high mirror shine of water gilding. But that problem has now been solved by the revolutionary Kolner Instacoll system.

This has been a revolutionary innovation in the world of Gilding, offering a solution to the challenge of achieving a high brilliant finish with transfer gold leaf, which was previously only possible with water gilding using loose-leaf gold.

Following are some key points about the system and its impact on the art of Gilding.

Innovation

The Kolner Instacoll system was developed in Cologne, Germany in 1979. It is a two-part water-based system that allows for the application of transfer gold leaf that gives a bright, highly reflective mirror gloss finish. This system bridges the gap between the ease of use of transfer leaf and the high-gloss finish of water gilding with loose-leaf gold.

Application process

This simple water-based system involves applying a basecoat followed by an activator topcoat, both of which are allowed to dry. The transfer gold leaf is then applied to the surface and gently rubbed with cotton wool. This process results in the gold leaf achieving a bright and highly reflective mirror-like finish.

Advantages

With this system, gilders can now achieve a mirror gold finish using transfer leaf, on both interior and exterior work, simplifying the gilding process and making it more accessible to a wider range of beginners, artisans and craftspeople. This innovation removes much of the complexity and challenges traditionally associated with traditional Gilding and the problems of achieving a high-gloss finish with transfer leaf.

Impact

The Kolner system represents a significant advancement in the field of Gilding, offering gilders an easier way to achieve a mirror-like finish without the need for traditional complex water gilding techniques and loose-leaf gold. This innovation opens up new possibilities for applications in various industries from furniture and the decorative arts to architectural ornamentation. Overall, the Kolner system has revolutionised the art of Gilding by providing a practical solution for achieving a high-gloss finish with transfer gold leaf, combining the best of both worlds in terms of ease of use and aesthetic beauty.

Step-by-step

GILDING

The finished piece.

MATERIALS

- masking tape
- Easy-Gild system
- fitch
- 24ct transfer gold leaf

Mask off the areas to be gilded. Apply Easy-Gild basecoat and allow to dry. Apply the activator and allow to set. These processes can be quickened with the help of a heat gun if required.

Cut the transfer leaf to size with scissors. Lay onto the surface, and with a shortened cut fitch, rub and press down. The gold should come off the transfer paper and adhere to the surface.

Remove the masking tape.

For design work, choose your design. For Gilding onto dark surfaces, chalk the reverse with white chalk. For light, use a graphite pencil. With an ink pen, draw over your design, transferring the outline onto the surface. Repeat step 2. Lightly rub the gold leaf with a cotton wool ball.

The gold will rub up to a bright, brilliant finish.

PART TWO GRAINING AND MARBLING

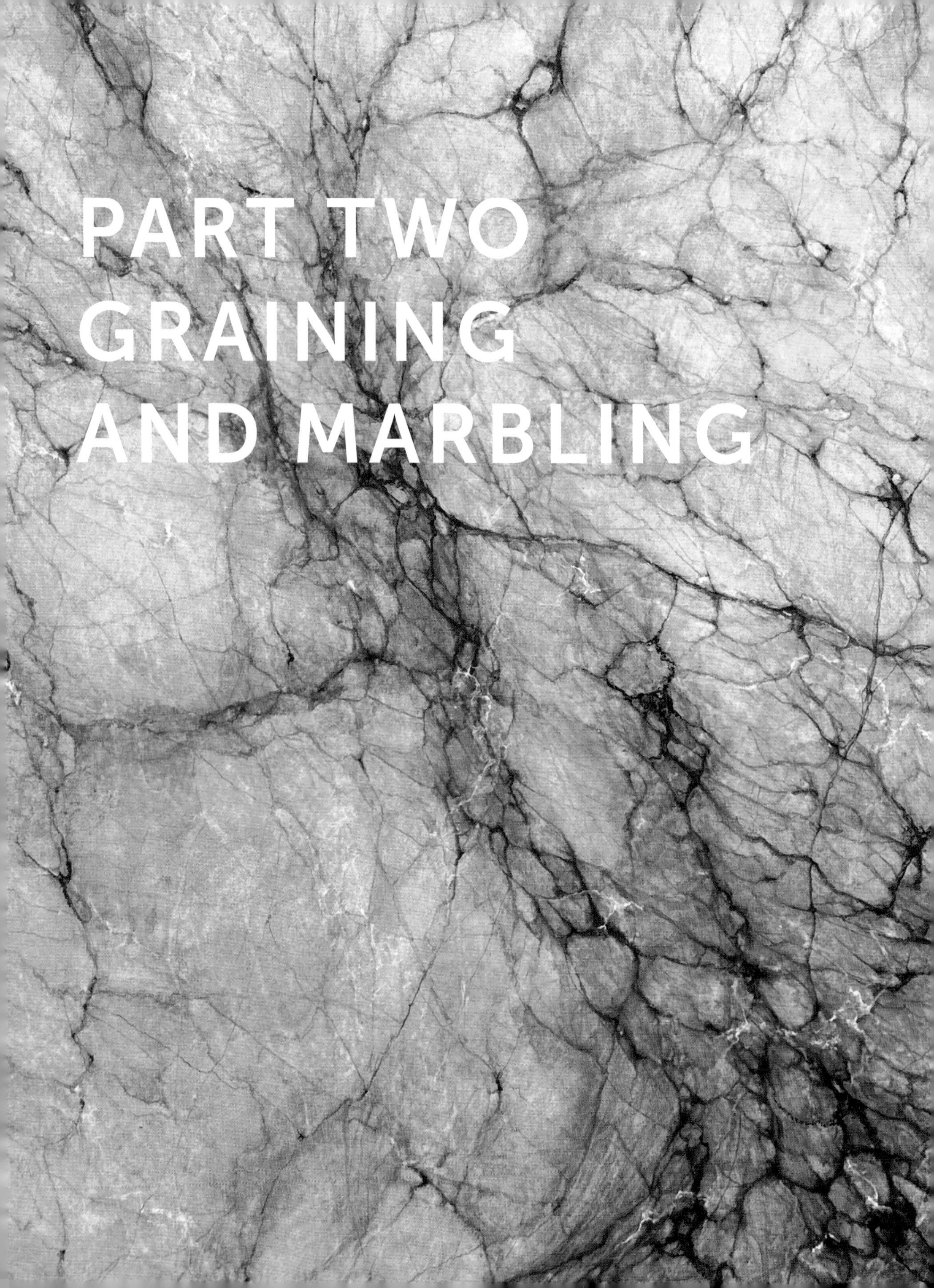

Before dealing with these two effects individually, it is important to look at them as a whole. Here in the UK, Graining and Marbling are considered to be the two main advanced craft skills expected of any qualified, competent, decorative painter. All good tradesmen were expected to have had some training and experience in Graining and Marbling (Graining especially). The two have always gone hand in hand, like two sides of the same coin.

However, because of the diverse nature of the techniques involved in the two finishes, painters would sometimes emerge favouring and being more proficient in one than the other. Here in the UK, as a young decorator, I found that it was Graining that was much more traditionally favoured and practised amongst the qualified tradespeople. I would serve my apprenticeship hearing mythical stories of legendary decorators of the past who could, in a matter of days, turn a plain, painted Georgian drawing room into a sumptuous wooden masterpiece, its previously plain white wainscotting now blooming in majestic, rare, quartered oak.

Day to day here in the UK, Graining was practised more by the decorator, and it was for this reason that for hundreds of years it gained a strong foothold and tradition, its tools and techniques passed from master to apprentice and from generation to generation. Marbling, by contrast, because of its almost regal quality, was more fabled and rarer amongst practising decorators. A decorator who could grain was feted as exceptional. But a decorator who could both grain and marble to the highest level was revered and could achieve almost godlike status in the trade.

The Paris Exposition and Great Exhibition of London in the Victorian era brought attention and acclaim to Graining and Marbling, catapulting its practitioners to fame and fortune in their lifetime, and creating a tradition that has been held to this day. The meticulous and secret artistry of Graining and Marbling, once confined to the skilled hands of a select few, was thrust into the limelight on the grand stage of these prestigious exhibitions. The legacy of these master craftsmen lives on, inspiring future generations of decorators and artists to continue the tradition of Graining and Marbling.

While the demands of modern taste and style are always shifting, the timeless appeal of these techniques endures.

OIL OR ACRYLIC

What and when to use?

Before setting off and plunging headfirst into advanced decorative painting, particularly Graining and Marbling, it is crucial to address a very important issue; one that, in recent years, has come more to the fore than ever before. Most of the paint effects in the previous chapters deal individually with the medium concerned with that particular finish. There are no set rules. Oil (linseed oil-based glaze or scumble) and acrylic (water-based glaze or scumble) can usually be chopped and changed, and used in accordance with the reader's preference, and one can usually be substituted for the other with no ill effect. I normally give a pointer of my preference of medium, which is usually a suggestion only.

Now this brings us exclusively to Graining and Marbling. Over the past decade or so, acrylic has become the exclusive medium of choice amongst the majority of decorative painters. This preference has sometimes been wrapped up in an environmental ribbon by some, that is, acrylic should be used because oil-based media is more harmful to the environment – a different debate for a different time. My issue is that acrylic media is now being pushed by many as the holy grail of decorative paint media. It is fast drying, good for the environment, and easier to use and clean up – great advantages all round.

However, what I would like to put forward is my experienced thoughts, after 30-plus years in the industry as a decorative artist. My first, last and only concern when it comes to paint and media used is driven by one thing – quality. That is the only thing that has ever mattered to me, and because of this I use oil, every time. I was taught in oil, I use oil and I teach in oil. Acrylic has its uses, and I do use it myself in the later stages of projects, as I will later explain. But when it comes to the field of decorative painting that I practise in, oil is better. This isn't just an opinion, it is fact.

Let me explain exactly why this is. First, the all-round quality is better. It gives you a smoothness, subtlety and slickness that acrylic does not. Its opaqueness, transparency when blended, its chroma whilst thinned and blended all outperform acrylic. Oil is also unsurpassed for the quality of tone and colour when mixed, and dries to a purer value of colour than acrylic. All of these advantages are critical for high-end Graining and Marbling. This has been a scientific fact accepted by artists and the artistic community for centuries, and is beyond question. Also, its slow drying properties give the decorative artist time to blend and figure properly, critical for beginners and professionals alike. There has been no job, panel or project ever done completely in acrylic, that wouldn't be better in oil. Think of all the great masterpieces of art in history you have ever seen. From Michelangelo to Turner, from Rubens to Rembrandt, all painted in oil. When realism is required, 100 per cent of them used oil, always; and if Graining and Marbling strives to be one thing above all, it is realistic.

Furthermore, when Graining and Marbling, there are certain techniques that are simply impossible to carry out in acrylics. Chief amongst these is a technique called cissing. This is a technique I have used extensively in this book, and without which a lot of the work featured simply wouldn't be possible. Cissing is used predominantly in walnut Graining, and almost all marbles. Cissing, half-cissing, dabbing with a spirit cloth, opening up with a fine brush, and so on; there are dozens of small, subtle techniques that I use in oil that simply cannot be done in acrylics.

Then we come to probably one of the most important processes in high-end Graining and Marbling. That is the 'setting up' of oil. This is an advanced technique that has been used by masters for centuries. It is very faintly touched upon in some classic books, but was first taught to me by my mentor and teacher, the late Bill Holgate, who was one of the finest grainers and marblers of his

generation. This is a technique where the first pass and figuring on a project is carried out; that is, say in oak, the panel is coated and combed. In Marbling, the panel is coated, veined and figured. Then you wait. Depending on the mix of scumble and driers used, the panel will, after time, begin to 'set up'. This means that it will go from very wet, to semi-dry (but still workable). This usually lasts for around an hour before it dries further and becomes unworkable. It is what I refer to as 'the golden hour'. During this time, quartered oak figuring becomes infinitely more clean, crisp and sharp. Half highlights become easier to wipe, more subtle and controlled. In Marbling, wiping and ragging becomes refined and minutely detailed, small amounts of coloured glaze can be removed, half removed, reapplied over the panel again and again, producing an infinite variety of multilayered effects. This cannot be done in acrylics. In the 1850s, Thomas Kershaw achieved this crafts apogee using oil, because of the advancements, lower costs and new wider availability of oil paint to decorators at that time. For the first time, 'lowly' house painters could grain and marble with the same paint media used by van Eyck, Titian, Rembrandt and van Gogh. Kershaw and his contemporary John Taylor wasted no time. Previously hindered by cheaper pigments, they exploded the craft, producing never-before possible grained and marbled masterpieces of form, colour and depth, and gained worldwide fame and fortune by turning our craft into a new art form. They took Graining and Marbling to its zenith; all using oil.

Unless we study, practise, learn and pass on the processes and techniques used by the old masters, I feel a fundamental quality of work will be lost forever. Of course, we must always embrace and welcome new skills and ways of working, but we must also simultaneously have a great passion and drive to re-learn and employ the old arts and crafts. It is an act of extreme folly to think we can apply so-called 'modern' ways and products to ancient tried-and-tested finishes and expect anything other than an inferior, substandard outcome. I feel the modern profligacy and exclusive use of acrylics in Graining and Marbling is an extremely damaging and retrograde step to our craft and, if continued, will ultimately be disastrous to high-end quality work and the craft outright.

We should be standing on the shoulders of giants, not falling off them.

It is for this reason I feel this book will hopefully be important to keep alive the old arts that I was taught. Many of the techniques here were taught to me by Bill Holgate, and had been handed down to him by many generations of craftsmen. This book includes these techniques, but also many that have been rediscovered and, in some cases, created by me. So I urge any reader here to use oil as I do, when I do, and particularly always when Graining and Marbling.

As mentioned before, this does not mean that I don't use acrylics; far from it. They have a very important part to play in all my projects. When I teach single day courses, or do single day demos, I will invariably use acrylics, (usually acrylic varnish as the scumble), as its quick drying properties allow me to demonstrate and teach multiple techniques in a very limited timescale. But when real quality of work is required on jobs, longer teaching courses or exhibition work, it is oil that I use every time.

The first application and figuring on my high-end work is by far the most important one, and I always use oil. Whether it is on a large onsite job, or an exhibition panel, the primary, major figuring and formation I carry out is always done in oil.

I have developed a set process over the years which I have perfected to give the best finish possible on any required job or assignment. It gives all my jobs and projects a structure and concrete formula to follow and adhere to. It always starts in oil and then finishes in acrylics. This is it.

My process

When it comes to Graining and Marbling, every project I do, whether it's a large trade job, or an exhibition panel, or even a sample or practice panel, has two main stages: the first is in oil; the second, finished in acrylic.

The first stage in oil is by far the most important. This is where the most crucial part of the job takes place. It is also the longest phase. The main part of the work is carried out at this stage, where the chief figuring and composition of the piece is carried out. The longer drying time of oil facilitates the longer working time required, which in turn aids quality. It also allows me to carry out the various techniques described previously in 'the golden hour'.

Once this is dry, the remainder of the work is then carried out in water-based acrylic.

I use this oil/water process, as it allows me to get any reasonably big or small job finished technically in two days minimum. The work in acrylic is predominantly the detail of the work – things such as overgraining and overglazing, mottling, strié, fine veining lines for Marbling, and so on. These processes can be done very quickly, which suits the quicker-drying acrylics. I have found that there is no noticeable reduction in quality at this stage doing this type of work in acrylics.

On some of my smaller jobs, I often use an acrylic varnish as a medium at this stage, as this dries lightning fast, with immediate non-reversible qualities that expedite completion of the work with a final coat of varnish. However, this should only be attempted by the very experienced, for it is almost instantly non-reversible.

So, in conclusion, although acrylics have their uses, and average quality works and projects can be successfully carried out using them exclusively, for me they are only suitable for the quicker, peripheral aspects of Graining and Marbling. By all means, use them for practice if you are a beginner and want to. But always remember, when Graining or Marbling, practising will only get you good at practising; the goal should be completion. The best work you can possibly achieve from start to finish must always be sought. For the beginner, professional, or seasoned grainer and marbler who wants to achieve his or her best work possible, it must be oil. It is simply better in every way than acrylic.

If you are a serious decorative painter, the question should always be: do I want what's easiest, or do I want what's best?

THE HISTORY OF GRAINING AND MARBLING

The art and history of painted decoration has been a fundamental aspect of human culture for centuries. From the rudimentary to the sublime, it ranges from basic cave paintings to the almost heavenly Italian frescos. The journey of decorative painting is filled with innovation, expression and endless creativity. It goes back to the earliest cave artists who used paint derived from powdered earth and plants to depict scenes of hunting and day-to-day living on their walls, and the need for humans to paint their interiors has been present since that earliest desire to embellish our surroundings.

These primitive urges have developed and shaped art and design throughout human history. From Stone Age caves to the elaborate decorations of ancient Egyptian tombs and the intricate painted wall designs of Herculaneum and Pompeii, paint has been used both to escape banality and create luxury.

During the Middle Ages, art and decoration received significant patronage from the church with numerous murals and wall paintings commissioned for churches and cathedrals. This tradition was subsequently adopted by the nobility, who adorned their castles and stately homes with comparable artistry and tapestries, and this tradition fed down to the common home. The development of international trade in the seventeenth century facilitated an exchange of diverse and valuable artefacts and design ideas, bringing with them new decorative directions and styles from around the world. The implementation of Marbling in interior house decoration can be traced back to Egyptian and Roman times. This was not driven by the unavailability of the stone, but rather the impracticalities associated with its weight, transportation and brittleness. This tradition survives to this day, with Marbling and its faux twin Graining being used wherever cost or convenience will not allow. In 1856 Owen Jones wrote in his now famous book, *The Grammar of Ornament*: 'Imitations of woods and marbles are allowable in all cases where the real wood or marble would be used in construction by the architect.'

Advancements in paint technology have had a large influence on the painted finish and the painted home in general. For centuries painters had to rely on locally available pigments and hand-mixed paint, with their unique coatings, glaze mixtures and techniques held in high secrecy. This, more than anything, led to the term 'trade secrets'. The application of binders and drying agents such as egg white and glue size significantly improved the quality and performance of paint; however, colour variety and quality remained limited and evolved slowly over time. Improvements and changes were gradual, until the middle of the nineteenth century, when two major advancements collided, and produced a sudden acceleration and peak in the decorative arts which has seldom been equalled, even to this day. The first was the industrial revolution. The second was the paint tube.

In the mid-1800s, the industrial revolution was at its height with Great Britain at its centre, ruling the waves and the world's trade sea routes. Britain was then just 2 per cent of the world's population, but produced half of its manufactured goods. This resulted in a never-before-seen migration from rural dwellings to urban towns. These new booming mill, factory and shipbuilding towns in turn created a craft trade and apprenticeship explosion, and it is from these apprenticeships that came many of the world's most famous decorative artists.

The second advancement, the metallic collapsible paint tube, was developed by John Goffe Rand, an American artist and inventor living in London. He took out a patent on this idea in 1841 and began supplying them to the two largest paint manufacturers in London at that time: Rowney, and Winsor & Newton.

Mass production and sale of a reliable, portable, premixed oil paint was now available to the general public for the first time. Painters and decorative artists now had a ready supply of a quality oil paint, without the need for laborious, time-consuming and inaccurate hand mixing of pigments and oils. Almost overnight, the fine art and decorative painting world changed forever. For the decorative painter, systems, recipes and mixes could be perfected, recorded and shared. Previously complicated paint and scumble mixes could now be universally simplified, and much more importantly, relied upon. A whole industry and subsection of the decorating trade (Graining and Marbling) could now be properly learned, understood and, more importantly, taught and passed on. From this paint revolution emerged some of the most famous decorative artists to have ever lived, amongst them Moxon, Nichol, Bradley, Taylor, Sutherland and Kershaw. The list is long.

But above them all, one man stands astride the arena of decorative art and, indeed, the Victorian era like no other.

Thomas Kershaw (1819–1898)

Thomas Kershaw is widely regarded as the greatest decorative painter who has ever lived, and if ever there was a man made for his time, it was Kershaw. His Victorian zeal and ambition took him from a small farmstead in the Lancashire town of Standish, to the grand palaces of Paris and London. Gold medals, royal patronage, fame and indeed great fortune were all achieved in his lifetime. And all from the son of a humble farmer, and a lowly Bolton painter's apprentice. Kershaw's achievements are now legendary and woven into the very fabric of British painting and decorating, and decorative art: he won gold medals at the Great Exhibitions of Paris and London; he completed work for Queen Victoria at Buckingham Palace and Osborne House; he was made Freeman of the City of London, and personal painter and consultant to the richest man on earth at that time, Sir Anthony Rothschild.

Thomas Kershaw (1819–1898) was apprenticed in Bolton, England, and was arguably the greatest decorative painter of all time. He was a gold medal winner at the Great Exhibition of London (1851) and the Paris Exposition (1855). He has Graining and Marbling collections surviving in Edinburgh, Bolton and two in London.

It is hard to overestimate the impact Kershaw had then on decorative art, and still has to this day.

But why, in this mid-nineteenth century explosion of world-class decorative artists, did the Kershaw name rise above all others, and is still revered to this day? Is it purely a matter of quality? Having seen all the surviving examples of Kershaw's work over the years, I can contest to his truly breathtaking and seemingly unbelievable quality of work. But he did also have contemporaries of great ability; chief amongst them was Scotsman John Taylor, whose career ran parallel to Kershaw's.

Quartered oak graining on a panel, with Trompe l'Oeil strap work, gold leaf arabesque and fruit inlay, by Thomas Kershaw, c.1850.

Thomas Kershaw's gold medal from the Paris Exposition in 1855.

John Taylor [1826–1901]

Taylor was apprenticed to a painting firm in Glasgow, where he quickly displayed a strong artistic vein during his seven-year apprenticeship. On finishing his journeyman stage, Taylor, like Kershaw and most of the gifted painters of that time, soon gravitated to the 'place to be' for all the ambitious men of that time, London. He quickly gained employment under the famous designer J.G. Crace, where he soon secured a recognised position as his employer's chief grainer to the trade. Taylor also allied himself with prominent theatrical companies of that time, painting scenery and establishing himself with the leading scenic art companies and theatres of Drury Lane.

After a successful career in London, he moved and settled in Birmingham, where he set up a

John Taylor (1826–1901) was apprenticed in Glasgow, Scotland. He is often cited as an equal to Kershaw. Taylor was a member of the Royal Birmingham Society of Artists, and a gold medal winner at the Great Exhibitions of 1851, 1862 and 1870.

thriving business. A keen and successful pictorial artist, John Taylor was a member of the Royal Birmingham Society of Artists, and had works hung in Birmingham, Liverpool, Manchester, Bristol and the London Academy. His grained and marbled specimens were works of art in themselves, and won him gold medals at the international exhibitions of London, 1851 and 1870, and Paris 1862. He carried out work for Queen Victoria at Buckingham Palace, and also for The Prince of Wales (the future King Edward VII) and was awarded the Freedom of the City of London.

Brèche Violet Marbling on a column by John Taylor, c.1860s. (Photo courtesy of Neil Ogilvie, Chief Executive of the Painting & Decorating Association, Nuneaton.)

Of the work of John Taylor, there are only five specimens remaining: four half columns, approximately 1.25m (4ft) high marbled in Rouge Royale, Egyptian Green, Brèche Violet, and Irish Connemara, and one wooden panel marbled in Mexican Onyx. It is my opinion that these works could well be compared to, and are indeed equal in quality, to those of Thomas Kershaw.

This onyx marbled panel by John Taylor, c.1860, is widely regarded as the greatest example of Marbling ever executed in history. (Photo courtesy of Neil Ogilvie, Chief Executive of the Painting & Decorating Association, Nuneaton.)

Charles Moxon [1808–1891]

Another contemporary of Kershaw was Charles Moxon, 'The Royal Decorator'.

Apprenticed in Edinburgh, Moxon was one of the very first decorative painters to publish a book on the subject. *The Grainer's Guide* was published in Edinburgh in 1842 (where the National Museum of Scotland today holds one of the last few remaining copies). Moxon had successful businesses in both Edinburgh and London. He carried out Marbling in the Houses of Parliament, worked as house painter to Queen Victoria, and carried out many works at Buckingham Palace and Balmoral, earning him a royal warrant and his title 'The Royal Decorator'. He

Charles Moxon (1808–1891) was apprenticed in Edinburgh, Scotland. He was house painter to Queen Victoria and became known as 'The Royal Decorator'. He published one of the first ever decorative painting books, *The Grainer's Guide*, in 1842. He marbled the columns in the Blue Drawing Room at Buckingham Palace.

also carried out Graining work for Sir Walter Scott at his baronial home, Abbotsford, in the Scottish borders. He exhibited at the Great Exhibition of London in 1851, and beside Kershaw in Paris at the International Exhibition in 1862. In Paris, Moxon's work was discussed in the French decorative painting journal, *Journal Manuel de Peintures*.

The editor, a Monsieur Biziaux, himself a master painter, personally described Moxon's work as follows: 'As a painter, he is a remarkable industrialist. His marbles were done on slate, which are superbly done, amongst others a Sienna, which is truly incredible.' In summing up, he declares, 'None of the French painters has done work that can be compared to that of the English, neither in importance nor in talent as far as the woods are concerned, and we certainly have a lot to work on to be the same strength as the English.'

After being commissioned by Prince Albert to create marble columns in the ballroom at Buckingham Palace, in 1856 Charles Moxon was awarded a tradesman's warrant as Housepainter and Decorator to Queen Victoria.

These brief excerpts give a quick insight into the type of incredible company Kershaw was keeping at that time. So, the question remains: what exactly was it about Kershaw that resonates so completely to this day, and casts a shadow on his contemporaries? There are three factors: the quality of his work; his awards and recognition; and the actual work he left behind.

The third is by far the most important. Kershaw has left an incredible breadth and amount of work, in the shape of his exhibition panels, and indeed also the fantastic work commissions he carried out here in the UK, which still remain. His exhibition panels displayed at the Great Exhibitions in Paris and London remain intact. His work on the walls and pillars in Buckingham Palace and Osbourne House looks as good today as the day it was painted, and perhaps you could say even better with natural aging. He has over two dozen exhibition panels which are, with permission, still available to be viewed to this day. He has four collections residing in the UK, at the National Museum of Scotland in Edinburgh, at Bolton Museum and Art Gallery, at the Victoria and Albert Museum, London, and at The Worshipful Company of Painter-Stainers, in London. It is this that lifts Kershaw above all. His work, and lots of it, is still there for all to see. When viewed, it has the capacity to make you catch your breath, and is almost too astonishing to comprehend. It has become his extraordinary legacy. Like any great artist who leaves behind their great masterpieces, Kershaw has left his. As Leonardo da Vinci stated: 'Beauty perishes in life, but is immortal in art', and through his vast remaining collections of work, Kershaw more than any other decorative artist has remained alive, and it is this life that still inspires and influences painters to this day.

Conclusion

Kershaw, Taylor, Moxon and their contemporaries cast a long shadow indeed, but more than anything, it is one of inspiration. Kershaw's home county of Lancashire in England has produced a truly disproportionate amount of exceptional decorative artists throughout history, as a direct result of his work and legacy. I trained there also, my teacher and mentor himself being a Kershaw disciple. The history of decorative artists such as Kershaw and the painted finish itself is a rich one, which reached unimaginable heights in the Victorian era. From ancient caves to the dazzling palaces of Rome, Paris and London, it continues to capture the essence of the human imagination, each brush stroke and individual technique reflecting the spirit of its time. Despite vast changes in style over the centuries, the basic impulse behind decorative painting remains the same today as it was in Kershaw's era: the human desire to enhance our surroundings and express our identity, through the painted finish.

Charles Moxon, known as 'The Royal Decorator', marbled these pillars in the Blue Room at Buckingham Palace c.1860. (© Royal Collection Enterprises Limited 2024 | Royal Collection Trust. Photographer: Peter Smith.)

GRAINING

Graining is one of the oldest of the decorative painting crafts. It has been practised and perfected here in the UK for centuries, where its innovative, economical and functional popularity in the decorating trade ensured it quickly became established, and then rapidly spread to continental Europe and America. But it is eminently a British art, for it is in this country that it was first practised to its highest level and achieved its greatest popularity. All serious practitioners of our craft should study the work of Thomas Kershaw (*see* page 50).

The first forms of Graining were rudimentary until the mid-eighteenth century, when ships arriving from distant colonies of the British Empire brought with them their wares, including rare exotic foreign timbers. South American mahogany actually arrived from the Caribbean as ballast in the King's ships, until the ships' shrewd carpenters quickly recognised the hardwood's beauty and quality (and above all its value) when they turned it into furniture and carved goods. These rare new and expensive woods soon became much sought after by the upper class for doors, wainscotting and cabinet-making, and it very quickly became avant-garde for the rich. No home was complete without a piece of Chippendale mahogany. Sharp decorators wasted no time in filling the supply and price gap, and became experts in their imitation. With commerce now driving the practice, Graining quickly became a vital component of the British decorator's skill, and it became an established part of their apprenticeship and training. No decorator was considered accomplished unless he had learned and achieved some competent Graining skills. This practice continued from generation to generation, developing a great tradition of Graining here in the UK.

Graining today

Throughout the years, the popularity of Graining has waxed and waned with the ever-changing tastes and styles of interior home decoration and fashion. Unfortunately, here in the UK there has been a decline within the trade in its interest, and it is now rarely taught to young students and apprentices. This has produced a dearth of trained grainers, but ironically it now makes a good, skilled grainer worth their weight in gold. The market for Graining and grainers remains strong, which of course coincides with the market and desire for wood. The sheer beauty, richness and desirability of wood will never go out of vogue, with interior designers, architects and private clients always keen to include wood in some form or fashion in the home. As a means of decoration, wood has always been invaluable and sought after in all classes and types of buildings, both for interior and exterior decoration. The flexibility and economy of Graining has always run parallel to the tastes and fashions of real wood, and today, wood has never been more popular.

However, it is this very popularity and use that has now led to a modern environmental problem, a solution, and perhaps even an opportunity.

Due to man's insatiable desire for exotic and beautiful woods for building and decoration, over 7,000 of the world's most popular species of tree are now under threat. Incredibly, the very mahogany wood that was once used by British seafarers as ballast for their ships has now become endangered. Mahogany, teak, satinwood, rosewood and many others are now on the endangered list and protected, their harvest and use now banned. This has led to a unique opportunity for the grainer. With the beautiful forms, colouring and rich decoration of these once-abundant woods now protected and unavailable to anyone at any price, grainers are now in a position of being able to provide them.

And for the grainer? When painting one of nature's most beautiful gifts, whilst simultaneously protecting and conserving it, you've got to ask: is there truly a more noble or worthwhile craft in the world?

Modest oak woodgraining in a contemporary setting.

WALNUT BURR

Walnut is a firm staple that should always be in a grainer's repertoire. A beautifully rich, dark, dominant wood, it should be executed with some restraint and great thought in its placement. To many, Walnut Burr (referred to as burl in the US) is the most esteemed and decorative cut of wood in nature, and without doubt the cabinetmaker's prize, so rare that its twirling knots, mottles and grains are primarily reserved for luxury car dashboards, jewellery boxes and furniture. The beauty and workability of polished walnut has also made it a luxury favourite of guitar and piano makers for centuries. This dark, captivating wood is the crown jewel in the woodworking world, its depth of character and richness of grain setting it apart from all others.

Burr is so unique in nature that when it is discovered, it is more often than not cut into veneer form to maximise its utility.

For the painter, although Walnut Burr is best applied to door panels, countertops and other smaller areas of interest, the techniques and finishes shown here can easily be adapted to produce a straighter, plainer grain of walnut, which can be used in the surrounding sections of doors and projects.

The walnut tree is found throughout Asia, Europe, America and the UK. It is in Italy, however, that we find the finest examples of walnut wood and walnut burr, where the incredible depth and abundance of its swirling, speckled knots, juxtaposed and layered with its minutely mottled, undulating grain have no equal in the world of timber.

In nature, burrs are rounded irregular outgrowths on trees, and can be found on the trunks of many species, caused as a result of stress to the tree. These are quite harmless to the tree, and can become many feet in size after decades of growth. As burrs are extremely scarce in nature and can't be predicted or replicated, they are highly prized and valued when discovered. Some burrs can be hollow in places, and produce very little or no figuring, rendering them useless to the woodworker. It is this unpredictability and scarcity that gives walnut burr its great value when discovered.

The actual woodworking cut of burr is produced when these rare growths are sliced into, revealing its extraordinary figuring and pattern.

When graining Walnut Burr, the figure should be used sparingly, and in small areas because of the actual size of the burr in nature. Although burrs can occasionally grow very large, the average size is usually no more than 1.25m high × 1m wide (4ft × 3ft). It is for this reason that it is always best to grain burr in panels and smaller areas. Graining walnut burr demands precision and finesse. The main technique I use in the initial graining procedure here is carried out using cissing. This intricate process using oil and thinners brings out the knotty textures and

The finished piece.

variegated tones that characterise burr. It facilitates a natural opening up of the glaze and colour, giving a dramatic light and dark dispersion of glaze crucial to the contrasting elements of walnut burr. This technique can only be carried out in oil.

Step-by-step

WALNUT BURR

MATERIALS

- oil scumble
- acrylic scumble
- artist's oil paint
  - black
  - burnt umber
- artist's acrylic paint
  - black
  - burnt umber
- fuller's earth powder
- badger softener
- splayed paintbrush
- white spirit
- chamois
- hog hair overgrainer
- fan fitch
- 3-inch mottler

1

On an eggshell ground of light cream, apply a strong scumble mix of burnt umber, and with a cheap synthetic 1-inch brush, stipple all. Add a little black, and stipple in.

2

Using a synthetic brush cut down to a stub, dip it in white spirit. Shake off the excess, and flick a fine mist of spirit onto the surface, cissing all.

3

With a dampened chamois leather, rag roll the whole panel.

Start with the outer grain area of the burr. With a hog hair overgrainer lightly dipped in spirit, drag down one side. This is done with the brush at an angle, simultaneously pushing and cissing the glaze into the familiar walnut straight grain figure. Go over this grain again very lightly with the tips of the overgrainer, barely touching the surface, slightly twisting and turning as you go. Repeat several times. This will soften the grain slightly and produce the twisting, knotty abstract grain required.

4

5

With a soft fan fitch dipped in spirit, reinforce the outer edge of the burr figure by cissing and producing an irregular, lumpy edge.

With the same brush dipped in spirit, create the knots inside the burr. This is done by twisting and turning the very tips of the fan brush lightly on the surface, and moving and cissing as you go. Create islands of knots on the burr, with some sparce areas of knots connecting in between.

6

7

With the stubby 1-inch brush, dip it in the dark glaze and flick very fine spots onto the surface. *Very* gently, soften the panel with the tips of a badger softener. Also using the badger, stipple some areas very lightly as you go. Allow to dry.

continued on the following page...

Step-by-step

WALNUT BURR

... continued from the previous page.

Switch to acrylic paint. Degrease with fuller's earth. Mix a dark glaze of burnt umber and black. Starting on the outside, create mottles by coating the panel and rag rolling with a dampened chamois stretched between your fingers. This will add mottles, and also bring the shade value up to the centre burr area.

Soften with a badger. Allow to dry.

With a burnt umber glaze, coat the whole panel.

◀ Using a 3-inch mottler, mottle the whole panel. Mottle down across the outer grain at right angles, but the inner mottling can be curved around the knots. Smaller mottlers can be used on this area, including homemade mottlers made from rubber, cardboard and cork.

12

Soften all with a badger softener.

13

To add detail, using a pure black mix of *paint and water only*, highlight and apply grain structures around the knots and down the side grain. The most important part at this stage is to reinforce the *burr edge*, and to give a jagged, pointed appearance. This is achieved by applying black to the edge, then badgering in an outward direction only. As it dries, continue badgering and the paint will gather into rugged peaks, characteristic to burr outline grain. This technique should also be applied inside the burr knotty area to great effect, creating a myriad of small knots, islands and interconnecting grains.

MAHOGANY

Straight grain mahogany is the easiest wood in the world to grain. Mahogany feather, however, is not. With straight grain, a simple cheap paintbrush and a badger softener is all you need; simply get your scumble glaze coloured and mixed properly, and one of the world's most recognised and loved woods is at your fingertips. It is lightning quick to grain, looks rich and grand, and can completely change a room's atmosphere and look in minutes. The Mahogany Feather figure we do here is a bit more complicated, but it is very special. It is an undulating plume of rich, dark red flame, instantly recognised in door panels, cabinets and tabletops. Don't fear, however, as the figuring down each side of the feather in this panel can easily be adapted elsewhere for a straight grain application on doors or panelling.

Mahogany is so popular here in Britain that it has almost usurped English oak at the top of the nation's hierarchy of beloved woods, such is its beauty and versatility. It supplanted every other wood in the UK as the chief choice for cabinetmaking and furniture when it arrived. Never has a single wood changed a whole country's trade or interior like mahogany. It became so popular as a building and cabinet-making material in the late eighteenth century that 80 per cent of the wood imported into the UK was mahogany.

The first recorded mention of mahogany was by Sir Walter Raleigh, when in 1587 he noted in his ship's log the repair of the ship's rudder in mahogany when his boat was floundering off the coast of Trinidad. The history of its mass introduction into the UK some 100 years later is an incredible story, first documented by a Dr Gibbons, an eminent English physician of the 1690s. Wanting to make a box for holding candles, he asked his brother, a distinguished sea captain, if he had any exotic woods from his travels. His brother replied in the negative, informing him he only had a lot of large, unwanted foreign logs from the West Indies in the ship's ballast, but he could have them if he wanted. Have them he did, all delivered to his English garden. On making the box and finding the wood superior to anything he had ever used before, he asked his cabinetmaker if he could make him a new bureau from this mysterious wood. So pleased was he with the fine colour and polish when it was completed that he invited all his friends to see the new exotic masterpiece. Amongst them was the Duchess of Buckingham, who commissioned a bureau of her own from the same wood. The fame of mahogany was immediately spread, and sealed.

There is one cabinet and furniture maker, however, that raised mahogany to almost mythical status; arguably the greatest of them all, Thomas Chippendale. He took to the new wood like a duck to water, mahogany's lighter strength, beauty of colour, durability and ease of carving quickly making it his wood of choice, and allowed him to herald in a new revolutionary style in English cabinetmaking – rococo.

Painters wasted no time in filling the gap for the demand for mahogany, which at that time was only available to the rich, and the tradition of graining mahogany in British homes remains to this day.

There are many types of lower quality mahogany available today as a result of the species being cross bred, but historically the most famous for their striking beauty and colouring are those from South American Honduras, and Cuba. Of the two, Cuban mahogany is considered to be superior for its unique figuring, density and workability, and is considered the king of all the cabinet woods. Due to overharvesting to the point of near extinction, both species are now listed as endangered, and are not available at any price.

This scarcity gives the decorative painter an obvious opportunity to provide this beautiful wood to interiors where before it was once unthinkable and unavailable. The feather cut shown here is one of the most famous in the woodworking world, and is achieved by sawing into the intersection of the tree's branch and trunk.

The graining of mahogany is best executed where a rich, stately, elegant appearance is required, and looks particularly stunning on internal or external main feature doors. With the addition of a gilded trim, the results can be quite spectacular.

The finished piece.

Step-by-step

MAHOGANY

MATERIALS

- oil scumble
- acrylic scumble
- artist's oil paint
  - burnt umber
  - crimson red
  - black
- artist's acrylic paint
  - burnt umber
  - crimson red
- fuller's earth powder
- fan brush
- badger softener
- cotton rag
- fine sable brush
- fine calligraphy brush

1

On a bright yellow ochre ground, apply an oil scumble mix of burnt umber and crimson red. Add a touch of black, and coat the centre area. With the back of a brush, wipe a thin, wavy line down the panel. This will constitute the flow of the feather.

2

With a fan brush, begin wiping and figuring the feather, following your line from the centre out. Allow the natural shape of the fan brush to shape the feather, and at this stage form the whole, overall shape of the figure.

3

With the fan brush, pick up a little black, and define and darken some of the feather.

With a badger softener, soften all, running perpendicular across the grain.

With a brush end covered with cloth, wipe areas of the feather to create highlights.

With a fine sable brush, apply darker glaze to select areas to create definition and contrast.

Badger and soften all. Allow to dry.

▶ Switch to acrylic paint. Begin by degreasing the panel with a fuller's earth and water solution. Apply a dark glaze of predominantly burnt umber with a little crimson over the whole panel. Wipe some areas with a rag to create highlights and soften all. When dry, with a fine calligraphy brush, pencil in the fine grain lines that run across the figure, following its natural curves.

continued on the following page...

Step-by-step

MAHOGANY

... continued from the previous page.

With a soft fan brush, darken select areas with an umber and red glaze, and use the brush to blend this into the grain.

I finished the panel with straight grain mahogany marquetry separated by a faux boxwood inlay; 24ct gold leaf ornamentation completes the panel (*see* page 40).

ROSEWOOD

Rosewood is now the rarest and most protected wood in the world due to over-exploitation. Once abundant, this precious wood now teeters on the brink of extinction. The illegal rosewood trade has now made it the most trafficked form of flora and fauna in the world by value or volume. Its black market worth is now more than rhino horn and ivory combined. Known in many corners of the world as the 'ivory of the forest', the top two species of rosewood have now become unattainable, regardless of the price offered.

Nature's most precious and rare materials have always been a warm bedfellow for the decorative artist. The art of graining has always flourished when the real thing is unavailable or just too expensive. Historically, when exotic timbers such as rosewood were imported and started making their way into homes, they were generally the homes of the rich and elite. The graining of these woods would then be utilised by the painter to keep the less well-off aligned with the fashions of the times, and this practice became traditional and widespread. Even the aristocracy would employ the professional grainer to align their existing tired interiors and woodwork into the latest decorative styles at a fraction of the cost of the real thing with minimal disruption or remodelling.

There are many species of rosewood (called palisander on the continent), but the most famous are from India and Brazil. It gets its name from the deep red rich colour and sweet fragrance of rose incense when cut.

The graining of rosewood differs from any other wood due to its unusual undulating grain formation. These complicated veining structures appear to sprout suddenly like ribbons from under, over and around each other, appearing and disappearing from the sides, top and bottom. There seems to be no distinct arrangement, form or system to the grain markings. Most other woods have a regimented, recognisable framework of grain structure, but rosewood breaks all the rules. No other wood looks like it, the surface a seemingly tangled layering of heart grain and contrasting colours. This figuring and dramatic colouring can even sometimes make it resemble marble from a distance. Rosewood's colouring is showy and dramatic: jet blacks, dark cherry and purplish reds, juxtaposed with light creams and near white satins, which add further depth, with deep red purplish knots and heart grain creating a visual feast for the eyes. Without doubt, rosewood is one of the most distinct and beautiful woods in the world.

Even in Victorian times, rosewood was not abundant and even then, was relatively expensive. This made it an exclusive wood of choice for cabinetmakers. Today, the grainer can utilise it best on decorative inlay work, fireplaces, doors, spacious interiors and fine furniture. In inlay work it harmonises best with lighter woods such as bird's-eye maple, satinwood and boxwood banding.

In a world where true rosewood grows scarcer with each passing day, the art of graining offers a lifeline to its essence. By skilfully recreating the intricate patterns and colouring of rosewood, craftsmen can bring a touch of its opulence to a wider audience, preserving its beauty for generations to come. As we navigate a new landscape where conservation is paramount, rosewood serves as a poignant reminder of nature's fragility and the importance of safeguarding its treasures. Unlike our Victorian predecessors, the grainer of today is in a unique position to provide for our customer a wood that is not available to anyone in the world, at any price.

The finished piece.

Step-by-step

ROSEWOOD

On a light cream eggshell ground, coat the surface with an oil scumble mix of predominantly burnt umber, with just a little touch of crimson. With a coarse fan fitch, drag the grain vertically to produce a directional grain flow.

With the same brush cleaned and dipped in a little white spirit, begin to form the heart and outer grains. The cissing will produce the predominant strong grain ribbons characteristic of rosewood.

By angling the brush whilst cissing, strong shade variations should be created.

MATERIALS

- oil scumble
  - burnt umber
  - crimson red
- acrylic scumble
  - burnt umber
  - crimson red
- artist's oil paint
- artist's acrylic paint
- fuller's earth powder
- fan fitch
- white spirit
- round fitch
- cotton rag
- badger softener
- fine rigger brush

Step-by-step

ROSEWOOD

With a round fitch, pick up a little burnt umber, and begin darkening and accentuating areas.

With the same brush, pick up some lamp black and strengthen outer grain formations. Allow to dry.

Degrease the panel with a fuller's earth and water solution. Mix an acrylic scumble of predominately alizarin crimson and burnt umber, and coat the entire panel.

7

With a damp rag, semi-wipe out areas to create highlights.

8

Soften all with a badger softener.

9

With a very fine rigger brush dipped in black, accentuate inner fine heart grain areas.

10

With the same brush, strengthen the outer grain framework. Vary the thickness and flow of the grain by changing the pressure of the brush on the surface with a shaking motion of the hand. Allow to dry.

11

With a crimson and burnt umber mix, darken some heart grain areas. Extreme contrast should be the objective.

12

To finish, soften with a badger softener.

OAK

Quartered Oak and Heartwood Oak

In Great Britain, oak is more than just a type of wood: it is a symbol of strength, grandeur and endurance. To many, it embodies the very essence of the British national character. Throughout the centuries, poets and artists have sung its praises, extolled its virtues and celebrated its role in shaping British culture.

One of oak's most notable features is its remarkable range of colour and variety of markings. From light cool tones to deep rich browns and near black umbers, oak exudes a unique versatile beauty. Its distinctive grain patterns make it an ideal choice for imitation, a quality that has endeared it to craftsmen and designers alike for centuries. The enduring popularity of oak can be attributed to its durability and resilience. Used in the construction of ships, furniture and buildings, oak has earned a reputation for its strength and longevity. From the panelled wainscoting of ancient halls to intricate ecclesiastical carvings, oak has left an indelible mark on British architecture and design. What sets oak apart from other wood is its individuality. No two pieces of oak are alike, each displaying a distinct pattern of grain markings. This inherent uniqueness adds to oak's popularity and makes it a prized material for woodworking projects of all kinds.

As we look around us, whether it is at grand manors or humble cottages, we find oak in its natural form or meticulously imitated. Its warmth and character bring a sense of comfort and tradition to any home or space. Oak truly stands as a testament to the enduring spirit of British strength and beauty.

In the world of woodgraining, oak holds a special place in the British conscience as a wood that is both revered and universally appreciated.

The tradition of graining oak here in the UK is centuries old. From the never-ending list of truly great grainers of the past such as Kershaw, Taylor, Hay, Nichol and Moxon et al., graining English oak is an absolute British obsession. It is the gold standard, the definitive test, and the very epitome of a grainer's skill. It is the first and sometimes only wood students are taught to grain here, and by far the most difficult. It is the standard to which you are always held. To grain English oak really well is the ambition of every decorative painter in the UK.

For the purposes of this book, however, I have decided to forego a lot of the tools and methods that are usually and traditionally associated with graining oak. There are as many tools and techniques invented for oak as there are decorators using them. They have been exhaustively documented hundreds if not thousands of times in many books for well over a century. My aim is to give the reader a fresh insight into the graining of oak, methods which I have solely formulated and adapted from the many old, trade secret techniques that I was taught, and a few which I have developed myself. I have studied quartered oak graining intensely for over a quarter of a century, read every book on the subject, and

The finished piece.

was taught by one of the finest oak grainers of his generation. However, I was never completely happy, and decided to diverge, to forge my own path away from some of the traditional methods and techniques that were routinely taught. Rather than regurgitate old methods from other books, I offer an exclusive combination of the traditional and the new; an individual way of graining oak.

However, graining oak is hard – there is no sugar coating it. I have known decorators who have spent their entire lives trying to perfect it, and not even got close. Quartered oak in particular is the hardest of taskmasters. The wiping of the flakes or 'medullary rays' can take many years of practice. Oak heartwood, although not as difficult as quartered, can thankfully be adapted and simplified to a manageable level, whereas quartered oak cannot.

But there is hope for the beginner! Here I have included a workshop for graining both quartered oak and heartwood. With a little imagination, many techniques here can be adapted and applied to provide a much plainer, simpler finish. Also, I have included some very simple exercises in different oak combing techniques which, on their own, can produce some fantastic oak finishes.

Step-by-step

QUARTERED OAK

MATERIALS

- oil scumble
- acrylic scumble
- artist's oil paint
  - burnt umber
  - black
- artist's acrylic paint
  - burnt umber
- fuller's earth powder
- veining horn
- chamois
- cotton rag
- steel comb
- microfibre cloth
- soft makeup brush
- badger softener
- 3-inch mottler
- steel comb

1

◀ On a bright cream/ochre ground, apply a 'tight' coat of oil scumble, mixed with burnt umber. This coat should be strong in oil paint, with little scumble. It is imperative that this coat is brushed on thinly, and quite dry in nature. This extreme, tight coat is called 'rubbing in' in graining circles and is one of the vital keys to good oak graining work. The single biggest mistake in oak graining is caused by putting too much scumble onto the surface at the start, resulting in wet, sloppy, muddy work. Traditionally, after this coat is applied, it could be allowed to 'set up' for a period depending on the scumble mix, which provides even crisper figuring when worked.

After rubbing in, start wiping the figure from the top of the panel. At this stage I use a wiping tool that I have specially made from carbon steel, specifically for graining quartered oak. I fashioned it with a small, flat edge at the top, which helps me achieve the italic qualities of the quartered flakes as I wipe. The larger flatter sides and bottom of the tool I use for the larger wiped figuring. A round shoehorn was traditionally used, but I have always found these inferior. With the tool wrapped tightly in a chamois leather, begin to wipe the figure. It is critical to shift the leather onto a clean spot after every single wipe, to ensure clean, sharp work. Follow the pattern down, concentrating on the large figuring at first to create flow and pattern, then go back over the figuring, filling in with smaller flakes and detailing. At this stage, I use a sketchbook of quartered oak patterns which I have drawn over the years. I find this invaluable in the graining of quartered oak.

With the bottom of a one-inch steel graining comb wrapped in a microfibre cloth, gently press down between larger areas of figuring, to create half highlights. The edges of some of the figuring can be touched and incorporated into this technique to produce subtle blending. The wiping tool should *always* be held horizontal to the panel during this phase of Graining.

A selection of tools for wiping English Quartered Oak with a chamois. Traditionally, these were made by the grainer from shoe horn, but I have developed my own (top) fashioned from carbon steel, which I find to be infinitely superior, and more adaptable.

continued on the following page...

Step-by-step

QUARTERED OAK

… continued from the previous page.

Using a soft, cheap makeup brush, gently blend these half highlights more into the figuring. This brush can also be used at this stage to create smaller areas of blending between the small, tighter areas of the flake figuring. Allow to dry.

◀ Switch to acrylic paint, and degrease with fuller's earth. Using a sword liner, paint in the individual vertical grain Strié with a glaze of burnt umber. Vary the width from wide to narrow as you progress. For commercial Graining, coating the panel and combing with a notched rubber comb is a popular method at this stage, and less time-consuming, but this method darkens the panel considerably and is unsuitable for exhibition work.

6

Using the finest metal graining comb you have available, cross comb the Strié. This breaks up the lines to give an authentic oak broken grain look, and should be done at an 80 degree angle. Allow to dry.

7

Mix a glaze of burnt umber with a little black. Coat the panel, and with a dampened rag pinched firmly between the points of your fingers, wipe down the panel, following the flow of the Strié. Use the same bit of rag each time as you wipe. As the glaze builds up on the rag, it should simultaneously wipe bands, but also leave minutely fine vertical lines down the panel, which are characteristic of oak. Lightly soften vertically with a badger. Allow to dry.

8

Now we turn to mottling. Mottlings on wood are soft, blended shadow lines that run perpendicular to the natural woodgrain. They can be either very soft and faint, or bold and dramatic, and they are always a very effective and easy way to achieve a striking 'woody' effect when graining. There are many techniques and brushes used to achieve this look. For this, I use the same scumble mix and technique as described in step 7, only the wipe is done horizontally, and in a more broken, varied, random manner.

continued on the following page...

Step-by-step

QUARTERED OAK

... continued from the previous page.

9

To finish, quickly and very softly badger along these lines in the same direction, then finish them by going gently across them, blending them softly into the panel. The mottling on quartered oak should not be showy, but should just leave a faint impression across the grain.

Step-by-step

HEARTWOOD OAK

1

◀ For the heartwood, rub in the panel with the same scumble mix as you used for quartered oak. Using the reverse end of a pointed wiping tool, score a faint line from the bottom upwards in a slight undulating motion. Reverse the tool, and using the wiping end, begin wiping the heartwood figure. As you commence wiping, if care is taken to ensure the very tip of your wiped figure hits the score line, then the figure will automatically progress up the panel with some movement, and possess a natural flowing look when completed.

Continue up the whole panel, and proceed wiping down each side. The wiping should be quite wide from the centre, then progressively tighter as you move towards the edge.

Using a fine steel comb, cross comb upwards at an 80 degree angle. Allow to dry.

Switch to acrylic paint, and degrease with fuller's earth. Coat the panel with the same acrylic glaze mix used for quartered oak. Get any old wooden fine paintbrush and sharpen the end to a point. Cover with a chamois leather and wipe the heartwood figuring, just below the heart grain. With a fine rigger brush and some burnt umber glaze, emphasise the heart grain. Badger all softly in an upward direction. Wipe some quartered flakes down the side and around the heart centres.

continued on the following page...

HEARTWOOD OAK

... continued from the previous page.

◀ With a 3-inch mottling brush, mottle down the sides of the panel. This is achieved by pressing the mottling brush firmly onto the wet glaze and moving down the panel. As you go, press and release the pressure on the brush repeatedly. The brush does not leave the surface, but the variations in pressure as it moves down leaves a distinct striped silhouette across the surface of the grain. These mottles should be down the sides only, be quite sparing, and never go across the heartwood.

To finish, badger in the same direction of the mottles first, then across them, blending them into the grain slightly.

ENGLISH OAK COMBING EFFECTS

Below are some combing examples that can be used for producing the straight woodgrain of English oak. Whole doors can be combed with these examples to great effect, either individually or combined. The very best and cleanest combing for top or exhibition work can be produced when the oil scumble has been left to 'set up' (very partially dried) for a period of time, usually around 30–60 minutes prior to combing.

These exercises below can be carried out in acrylic, but are best done in an oilscumble, for quality and extra open time. The wiping and combing can be interchanged and mixed, to produce many different effects. I have carried this exercise out here on a white ground for visual contrast, but it is traditionally carried out on a light cream/ochre ground.

First, apply an oak scumble mix to the surface, and whilst wet apply both techniques – A, quickly followed by B.

ENGLISH OAK COMBING EFFECTS

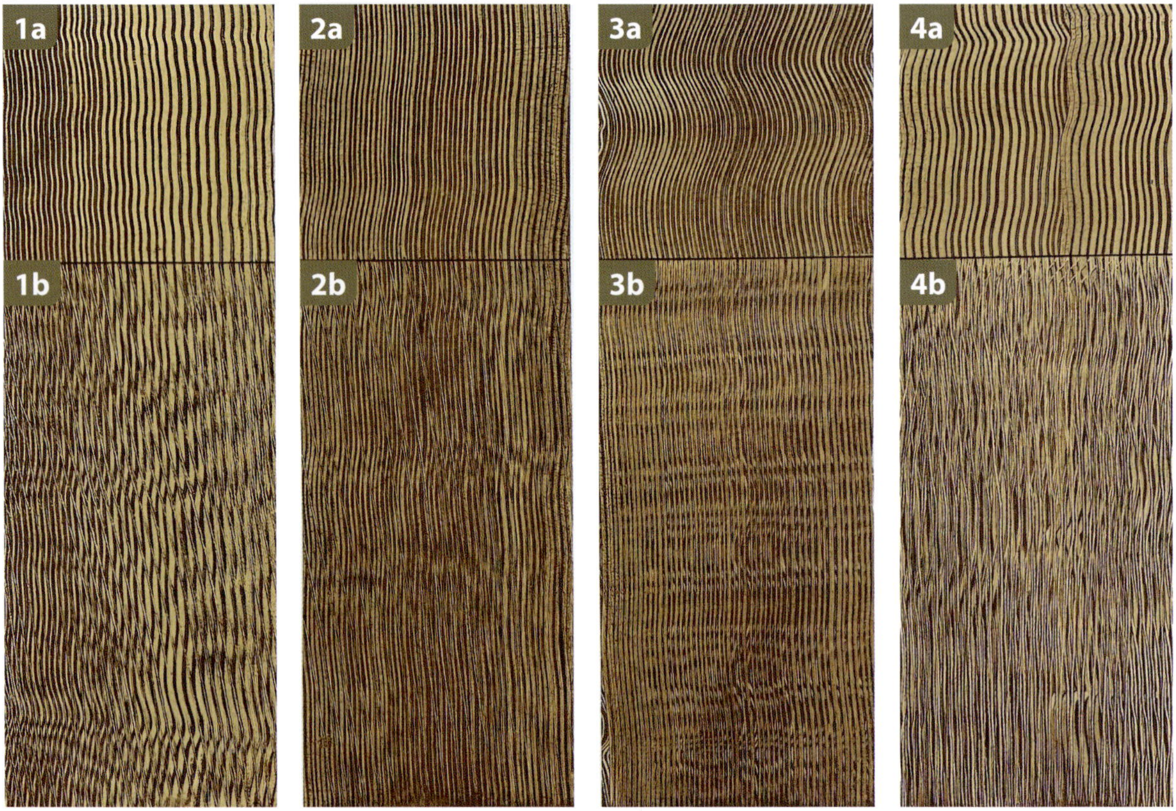

1a. Wide spaced rubber comb (graduated notches), vertical wipe.

1b. Cross combed with a fine steel comb at 80 degrees.

2a. Fine spaced rubber comb (graduated notches), vertical wipe.

2b. Cross combed with a fine steel comb at 80 degrees.

3a. Fine spaced rubber comb (even notches). Vertical wavy wipe.

3b. Vertically combed over with a fine notched rubber comb.

4a. Medium spaced rubber comb (even notches), slight vertical wavy wipe.

4b. Vertical wavy combed with a fine steel comb.

MATERIALS

- rubber combs
- steel combs
- cork
- hessian cloth
- rattan matt

5a. Cork pad (random notched) vertical wipe.

5b. Cross combed with a fine steel comb at 80 degrees.

6a. Folded hessian pad, vertical wipe.

6b. Crossed combed with a fine steel comb at 80 degrees.

7a. Folded hessian pad, vertical wipe.

7b. Slight wavy vertical comb with a fine steel comb.

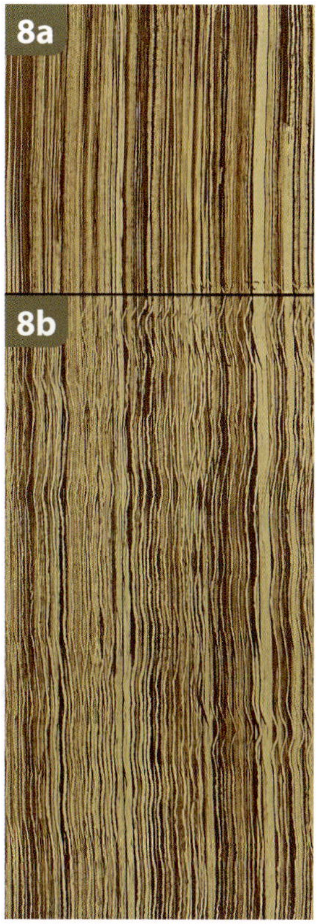

8a. Rattan matt, vertical wipe.

8b. Slight wavy vertical comb with a fine steel comb.

MARBLING

Marbling is the oldest of the decorative arts. Nature has been extremely generous with its gift of marble, the earth producing a seemingly endless variety from all corners of the globe. Within these varieties, there have emerged chosen staples, widely sought after by artisans and architects for their timeless appeal, and preferred by many cultures for their dazzling colour, designs and markings.

The exact date humans first reproduced marble with paint is not known, but the first recorded examples were found in the ruins of Pompeii in Italy. These examples were dated to the seventh century BC, and for thousands of years since, man has attempted to capture the translucent beauty of marble in all its forms and hues. Although marble can be found in most of the world's continents and countries, it is in Italy where the most abundant and beautiful species are to be found. Augustus Caesar, the first emperor of Rome, famously said, 'I found Rome a city of brick, and I leave her a city of marble.' This established Italian marble as the most prestigious of all building materials and has been synonymous with opulence and wealth ever since.

Initially, painted marble was used in Italy where the natural stone would have been impossible or too costly to use, that is, concave structures, domed or vaulted ceilings, or large expanses of upper wall areas. The sheer weight of the natural material made its use prohibitive. The painter was therefore employed to simulate the marble beyond its natural limitations, ensuring decorative continuity where desired. However, as the painter's skill became more advanced, Marbling then became desirable in more focal areas such as columns, architraves and lower wall areas.

As the fame of Italian marble spread worldwide, so did its desirability amongst the great cities of the world. No grand hotel in London, Paris or New York was complete without Italian marble. Of course, such desirability then produced extreme scarcity and cost, with this problem then being solved ingeniously by the decorative painter.

Over time, the decorative artist's skills and techniques evolved in conjunction with the advancement of paints and media. This progression of quality and expertise now allowed existing palaces, stately homes, castles and cathedrals to have luxurious and exotic marble where it was never before feasible, on previously painted walls and surfaces, and all at a fraction of the cost of the real thing.

Ironically, the art of Marbling stagnated somewhat in Italy, where it remained firmly in the 'fantasy' category. It was in Western Europe that the Marbling torch was firmly taken up, with Scandinavia, Holland, Belgium, France and the UK eagerly elevating the craft to an art. It was here in the UK that Marbling reached its zenith, where John Taylor and Thomas Kershaw achieved never-before-seen heights in painted marble (*see* page 49).

Portoro marbling (*see* page 96) on a plaster column, with gold leaf gilding (*see* page 42) on the capital and base band.

MARBLING TODAY

Today, owing to the scarcity and cost of the real thing, Marbling has never been as popular. Some of the classic marbles featured in this book have been quarried to near extinction and are now put firmly into the 'antique' category. The Sienna type featured in this book carries this distinction. Although still available and being quarried, only pale, lighter-veined varieties are now available. The egg yolk, dark umber/black-veined varieties have been quarried to exhaustion and are not available at any price. The rare Portoro marble also featured here is now one of the most prestigious and expensive marbles in the world, coming in at £1,500 per square metre.

Marble is, above all, synonymous with luxury. When Marbling, whatever the setting, whether it be home or palace, it should never be understated. Marble is not part of a decorative colour scheme; it is a decorative feature within itself. When you paint marble, try and remember you are painting a mini portrait of the earth itself; millions of years of development, amalgams of pressure, fissures, fluids, minerals and sediments. It has all been quarried, cut, polished and pedestalled. It mustn't look as if it was painted yesterday, but is a product of eons. It must look both abstract and flowing, unhuman, forged by the earth and reflective of one thing above all – time.

CARRARA

The painting of Carrara is ostensibly an exercise in dots. It is the most ubiquitous of all the painted marble finishes, but also the most botched. Carrara, like all marble, has its own distinct features, unique to it alone. The mistake most decorative painters make is to produce a stock white/grey veined marble and call it Carrara. This is wrong. True Carrara is made up of a matrix of dots, ranging in size and strength, some distinct and boldly close to the surface, and some diffused, sunk and dispersed into the body of the marble. These dots are often interlinked to form delicate veining close to the surface, complemented with a smattering of singular specks and blots.

These dots are actually made up of shattered zinc mineral fragments, embedded into the marble during its formation, and as a whole create a white aesthetic that is highly sought after in the design world. The beauty of Carrara for the decorative artist is in its versatility. It can be as plain or as complex as the painter desires, making it a terrific gateway marble to learn and practise.

It is by far the most abundant marble on earth, with a rich history and enduring appeal. It has been quarried in the Apuan Alps above the town it is named after since Roman times, from where around 1 million tons a year are now exported.

When the Roman emperor Augustus declared: 'I found Rome a city of bricks, I left her a city of marble', that famous marble in question was Carrara. It is indeed the most famous marble on earth, the most abundant, but surprisingly one of the most expensive. Due to its shimmering white beauty, Carrara has always been associated with pure pristine luxury, and is the premium marble of choice for architects, builders and designers. The world quite simply can't get enough of it. Carrara's sheer popularity and desirability has made it one of the most sought after and expensive marbles in the world, despite being so plentiful.

It comes in many grades, but the two main ones are Statuario and Carrara Bianco. Statuario, the purest and whitest, unblemished by any veining or colouring, has been highly prized by sculptors such as Michaelangelo and Bernini throughout history. It is responsible for some of the greatest works of art ever created. Unfortunately, these pure, unblemished deposits are now mostly exhausted.

The other class is Carrara Bianco. This is ours. The abundant, light grey veined type, is much sought after as a sign of luxury and wealth around the world and extensively imitated by decorative artists, beginner and expert alike. Carrara Marbling is extremely versatile, and can be executed anywhere a bright, white deluxe finish is required.

When rendering veined marbles such as Carrara, I always use a swan feather. There is no other tool available that gets anywhere near it for giving multifaceted broken veining so quickly, expertly and perfectly. When wielded with dexterity, experience and finesse, nothing can match it. It should always be the tool of choice when rendering broken veining. Also, the tip of the feather, when used softly, carefully and with restraint, can give fine, detailed veining. I use it here in conjunction with the pointed side of a sea sponge, which gives the dots that are integral and crucial for this particular stone.

The finished piece.

Step-by-step

CARRARA

MATERIALS

- oil scumble
- acrylic scumble
- artist's oil paint
  - lamp black
  - white
- artist's acrylic paint
  - black
  - white
- fuller's earth powder
- badger softener
- splayed paintbrush
- white spirit
- chamois
- cotton rag
- sea sponge
- swan feather
- calligraphy brush
- fine rigger brush

On a white ground, mix a dark oil scumble using lamp black and white. Using a cheap splayed synthetic brush, stipple the whole panel. Picking up a little black on the brush, stipple darker areas in the middle and towards the bottom of the panel. We are looking to create the basic structure and formation at this point.

Using a cotton rag slightly dampened with water, begin to both dab and rag roll the colour. As you progress, you should start to pick up some colour onto your rag and redeposit it onto the surface, creating a multitude of effects.

continued on the following page...

Step-by-step

CARRARA

... continued from the previous page.

With a slightly damp natural sea sponge, pick up some of the dark glaze from your tray on the pointed end of the sponge and lightly stipple the panel. Slightly turn the sponge as you go, to avoid pattern repetition. Start this process at the darker areas of the panel, working out.

Soften all with a badger softener. When softening with a badger softener, the brush should always be held at right angles to the panel, ensuring only the very tips of the bristles are meeting the surface. This is an extremely light, delicate process, but with experience can be done very quickly.

With a swan feather dampened with water, pick up some dark glaze and begin veining, starting at the darker areas of the panel. The feather should be predominantly pushed at this stage, opening up the feather vane, which in turn will create a myriad of veining effects. Periodically break some of this veining up by blotting with a rag.

6

Soften all with a badger, breaking up gently with the rag as you go.

7

Switch to acrylic paint. Degrease with fuller's earth, and with a glaze mix of light grey, coat the entire panel. Break up with a rag, wipe out some areas creating slight stone impressions and soften with a badger.

8

With a medium fine calligraphy pencil, begin to add detail with a strong grey mix. Accentuate some of the veins, add other fine, interconnecting veins, and strengthen some of the dots. When I am carrying out this detailed work, I always have a brush in one hand, and a damp rag in the other. The rag should be used to break up the veining. This is crucial to achieve an authentic marble vein look. Very lightly soften the dots, but not the veining. Allow to dry.

9

With a pure white glaze mix, stipple the whole panel with a sea sponge. Soften, and highlight some larger stone areas with a rigger.

10

To finish, soften all, and put in some final, very fine detail with grey.

PORTORO

Portoro (sometimes called black and gold) is one of, if not *the* most striking marbles in the world. Its light honey-gold chainmail veining weaving across a sleek velvet midnight black background is a classic, enchanting combination which has inspired craftsmen, poets and even musicians for centuries. When polished, this intense black surface looks as if liquid gold has been poured directly over it. It is one of the most prestigious and expensive marbles in the world, and used extensively for luxurious and opulent interiors and ornamentation. It is also the most distinctive and unique black marble in the world, and its exclusive characteristics and markings makes it easily distinguishable from any other stone, and each slab is like a mini masterpiece of black and gold art.

Quarried in Porto Venere in northern Italy since Roman times, Portoro, like many prestigious marbles, comes in different grades, with the highest and most expensive being the ones that boast predominantly gold veining. These premium slabs are particularly rare and valuable in part due to the challenging extraction process which is near the sea, leading many quarries to cease operation as the stone becomes increasingly scarce or depleted.

For the craftsperson, having Portoro in your armoury is a very useful weapon to have. A fundamentally quick and dazzling marble to execute by the painter, it has been a favourite of decorative artists for centuries. As it is so dominant and eye-catching, large wall areas are usually avoided as it can be overwhelming, but I have seen whole bathrooms clad in it. The finish was admittedly stunning, and if a sensory overload was required, it was most certainly achieved. It is more traditionally used for ornamental focal points such as columns, fireplaces, bathroom and kitchen tabletops, any ornamentation and inlay work, or wherever a stunning focal point of elegance is required.

Portoro is a great marble for the beginner and experienced painter alike. A fantastic-looking imitation can be achieved really quickly once the basic techniques and colouring are mastered. I have used it many times from large columns to smaller items of inlay and ornament, and nothing less than a spectacular finish was ever achieved. It also works really well juxtaposed with other marble, contrasting particularly brilliantly with its white Italian cousin, Carrara. Care must be taken with the veining, though, as it is easy to get over-elaborate, and the form can be lost. With this stone, the chain veining must stand out, like flowing ripples in a stream, sometimes connecting, but mostly singular, strong and independent. Balancing the intricate design elements can be challenging, but when executed correctly in form and composition, the marble's chain-like veins create a sense of flowing movement. Whatever you execute it on – a practice board, large installations, fireplace or column – one thing is always guaranteed: Portoro never fails to impress.

The finished piece.

Step-by-step

PORTORO

MATERIALS

- oil scumble
- acrylic scumble
- artist's oil paint
  - black
  - white
  - yellow ochre
- artist's acrylic paint
  - black
  - white
  - yellow ochre
- fuller's earth powder
- badger softener
- splayed paintbrush
- white spirit
- calligraphy brush
- cotton rag
- fine rigger brush
- round fitch

1

On a black eggshell ground, wipe the entire surface with a thin film of clear scumble. This helps and dramatically improves cissing. With a medium long Chinese calligraphy pencil, begin to put in the vertical veining. On your tray, mix a strong yellow ochre glaze, and separately mix a pure white one. Load your brush with mostly ochre on one side of the brush and a little white on the other. Beginning at the top, roll the brush down the surface, gently pressing and easing the brush on the surface as you roll down. This creates the distinctive chain mail veining effect of Portoro.

▶ For cissing, cut a cheap 1-inch synthetic brush down to a stub. Dip it in white spirit, and flick off the excess spirit. Begin flicking the spirit over the entire panel. The veining will begin to ciss. To control the cissing and to stop it if required at any point, gently press with a dampened soft rag.

2

Continue down the panel until you have achieved a series of bands. It is important at this point not to paint too many bands, as Portoro is characterised by black gaps, pockets and openings.

3

With a small round fitch dipped in spirit, open up many areas of different sizes, some round but mostly elliptical, creating openings in the vein structure. The cissing creates a strong ring of colour around these openings, which is very characteristic to this marble. With a very fine rigger, interconnect some of the veins, and add fine detail veining, creating small hollows. Allow to dry.

Switch to acrylic paint. Degrease with fuller's earth. Mix a very dilute, thin glaze colour of pure white and begin painting very fine veining between some of the large gaps in the vein structures. Soften all. Apply the same mix down one side over the veining to create visual interest.

Mix a strong yellow ochre glaze and reinforce focal areas. Using neat black and a small round fitch, 'direct paint' round and elliptical gaps in the chain-mail veining.

▶ Connect some areas of the large veining with smaller veins using the same glaze, slightly breaking some of these. Be careful at this point, as too much detail and fine veining can easily overwhelm the work. Always occasionally step back and look at the overall composition of your work in these later stages. Always remember, Portoro is predominantly a *black* marble.

To finish, using neat black with just a little glaze, apply it over one or two of the smaller vertical chain formations and blot them with a rag. This should tone them down slightly and cause them to recede into the background. This is crucial to the balance and overall look of the work.

BRÈCHE VIOLET

When it comes to marble for the decorative artist to learn, the Italian marble Brèche Violet holds a prestigious position among what can be considered the 'big four' alongside Sienna, Carrara and Portoro. I have included them all in this book. All are extremely rare, expensive or extinct, and are here because if the various techniques gained in learning them all are mastered, it should equip the decorative artist with the skills to paint any other marble of choice.

Brèche Violet is rare in that it gives the decorative artist a chance to master the famous Brèche Violet appearance of stones, in undulating form and colour, which sets it apart from other marbles. The Brèche part of the name signals the presence of flowing, soft, round stones of all shapes and sizes, giving it a unique aesthetic appeal. The colour palette ranges from light purples and greys to rich, deep, dark violets and purples. Although the term Brèche in Marbling is usually associated with any marble that has stones, the actual translation from French is roughly 'breach' or 'gap' – the breach or gap in this instance being the space in marble veining that forms the stone fragments and patterns. It is not to be confused with the Italian marble types of 'breccia' which contain sharper, more pointed angular stones. Although it is an Italian marble, it was quarried in northern Italy close to the border of France. When it was discovered, it was heavily imported into France, where it became famed, gaining its name and confusing French spelling. For the painter, Brèche Violet marble usually offers rounder, more flowing markings than its sharp breccia cousins. The rich violet colour is unmatched by any other marble, and it is this unique combination of colour and stone that has made Brèche Violet one of the most recognisable marbles in the world, and highly prized by decorative artists for centuries for its unique colouring and patterns.

A very striking marble, I have rendered it myself on many fireplaces and columns, and the finish is always opulent, elegant and rich. It is by no means a subtle marble, and must be executed with this in mind.

In the Victorian era it was highly sought after all over the world for its striking formation and dazzling colour, and its immense popularity in the fine stately homes and palaces of Europe led to its scarcity. Many famous decorative artists of the time such as John Taylor and Thomas Kershaw learned to reproduce Brèche Violet so perfectly and efficiently that it gained them worldwide fame and acclaim. Their stunning panels of Brèche Violet can still be viewed to this day, some 170 years later.

While no longer available in its original form, its antique status underscores its value as a fundamental skill to be learned by the discerning decorative artist. Brèche Violet marble stands out as a rare and distinctive gem amongst marble, offering decorative artists a chance to master this specific type of

The finished piece.

Marbling, with its unique form and colour. Its rich history, artistic legacy, and unbeatable beauty make it a prized addition to any decorative artist's repertoire. By studying and mastering the techniques of this marble, painters can acquire the skillset needed to paint any marble of their choosing, making it a cornerstone of artistic expression in their range of decorative painting. Brèche Violet is a centrepiece marble, hugely dominant, and if used in complementary inlay projects, it works best alongside plainer, lighter marbles such as Carrara, Greek Skyros or French Blue Fleuri marble.

Step-by-step

BRECHE VIOLET

MATERIALS

- oil scumble
- acrylic scumble
- artist's oil paint
  - black
  - white
  - yellow ochre
  - violet
- artist's acrylic paint
  - black
  - white
  - yellow ochre
  - burnt umber
  - violet
  - purple
- fuller's earth powder
- badger softener
- splayed paintbrush
- white spirit
- calligraphy brush
- cotton rag
- fine rigger brush
- round fitch
- fan fitch
- swan feather

On a white ground, mix an oil scumble of predominantly violet with a little black. With a cheap, splayed synthetic bristle brush, stipple all over. At this stage have a formation of the marble in mind, with lighter and darker areas.

With a fitch dipped in white spirit, begin to wipe out the stone formations, creating formation and flow. These areas should ciss prominently.

▶ With a rag moistened slightly in white spirit, gently dab or wipe areas, creating more stone shapes. We are looking for major controlled cissing all over the panel here, but also as the rag picks up some colour and deposits it, we are aiming to create broken colour effects *inside* the stones too.

With a coarse fan fitch dipped slightly in white spirit, stipple, and also flick a fine spirit mist between the larger stone areas, creating more cissed stone shapes. We are looking for a veritable riot of cissing and stonework here, literally hundreds of stone formations of all sizes.

With a small fitch dipped in spirit, wipe and reinforce some of the smaller stones. Be careful when doing the last few stages that the integrity and formation of the marble structure isn't compromised. This is very important. Allow to dry.

Switch to acrylic paint. Degrease with fuller's earth. Mix a glaze of yellow ochre with a touch of burnt umber, and coat the entire panel. Gently dab and wipe some stone areas, being careful not to remove the glaze completely.

Soften all with a badger softener.

With a medium-sized calligraphy pencil and a dark purple glaze, reinforce the connecting structure of the marble between the stones, softly breaking this up with a dampened cloth as you go. Allow to dry.

Mix a half-and-half glaze of yellow ochre and burnt umber. Coat the panel. With a damp rag, wipe and blot the surface, to create lighter areas. Soften with a badger.

continued on the following page...

Step-by-step

BRECHE VIOLET

... continued from the previous page.

With a long rigger brush and some very strong black, purple and umber glazes, paint some very fine veining between the stones, and also include some sparse connecting veins running across them. At this stage, incredible time can be invested, with multiform and prodigious detail the aim. Allow to dry. With some yellow ochre and a fine fitch, bring out some stones to create a tonal contrast in the overall look. Repeat this process with white, violet and burnt umber. Allow to dry.

Switch to oil paint. Mix a scumble of white with a very fine touch of yellow ochre. With a swan feather, apply this across the entire surface. This should mostly follow the flow of the marble but should sporadically cut right across some stone formations.

Blot with a damp cloth, and ciss all with a coarse fan fitch dipped very slightly in spirit. Soften very, very gently with a badger. Accentuate and connect some individual veins with pure white and a rigger and make some veins really prominent. Allow to dry.

Switch back to acrylic paint and antique some stone formations by applying a glaze of yellow ochre, breaking up with a damp cloth as you go. Continue this with burnt umber, and some with a mix of the two. Soften all to finish.

ANTIQUE SIENNA

In the world of decorative painting, the French marble Sarrancolin is often hailed as the king of marble. But every king needs a queen, and in this realm of beautiful metamorphic rocks, that queen undoubtedly goes by the name Sienna. Her dark grey to black veining and glowing egg yolk undertones flaked with white and grey have captivated admirers for centuries.

Sienna is quarried from the Tuscan town of Siena in Italy, following the tradition of some marbles being named after the town or area they are quarried from. The difference in spelling is a quirk, a mistake in recording made centuries ago but has somehow stuck. Although heavily veined, Sienna is technically classed as a breccia marble (a marble containing stones). There are many types of Sienna marble, the most famous being the one I have painted here (dark-veined Antique Sienna), which was quarried from the sixteenth century, and now adorns many of the world's mansions, palaces and cathedrals.

Its close twin, Convent Sienna is even rarer, a treasure quarried close to the town of Siena and named after the convent of Montarenti, which owned the grounds it was quarried from. It is almost identical to Antique Sienna, but boasts the addition of lustrous velvety ribbons of purple and violet veins, with subtle shimmering lilac undertones, offering a touch of exclusivity that is truly unmatched.

Antique Sienna is a historic marble (hence the prefix 'antique'), which means it is quarried no longer or with a very limited output. The Sienna available today has very little or none of the dark grey to midnight black veining of its predecessor. This makes Antique Sienna a veritable blockbuster for the marbler, who is now in the position to provide something which is not available from nature at any price.

Painted Sienna is extremely versatile, seamlessly blending into large wall areas, fire surrounds, columns or even fine pieces of ornament and tabletops.

Any serious students of Marbling should study Kershaw's Convent Sienna Marbling that he executed on the walls of the staircases of Osborne House on the Isle of Wight for Queen Victoria and Prince Albert in 1851. An almost unbelievable piece of craftsmanship which still looks incredible to this day, it must be considered as the single greatest piece of commercial Marbling ever executed. A masterpiece to be marvelled at, it stands as a testament to Victorian genius and the timeless durability and popularity of the art of Marbling.

Today, in the world of stone, Antique Sienna marble has become synonymous with sophistication and rarity in the world's places of beauty.

Its exquisite aura and elegance serve as a reminder of one of nature's most precious bounties, which can once again be offered by the decorative painter. With its golden splendour, Sienna will stand out as a symbol of refinement and luxury in any decorative or architectural schemes and applications.

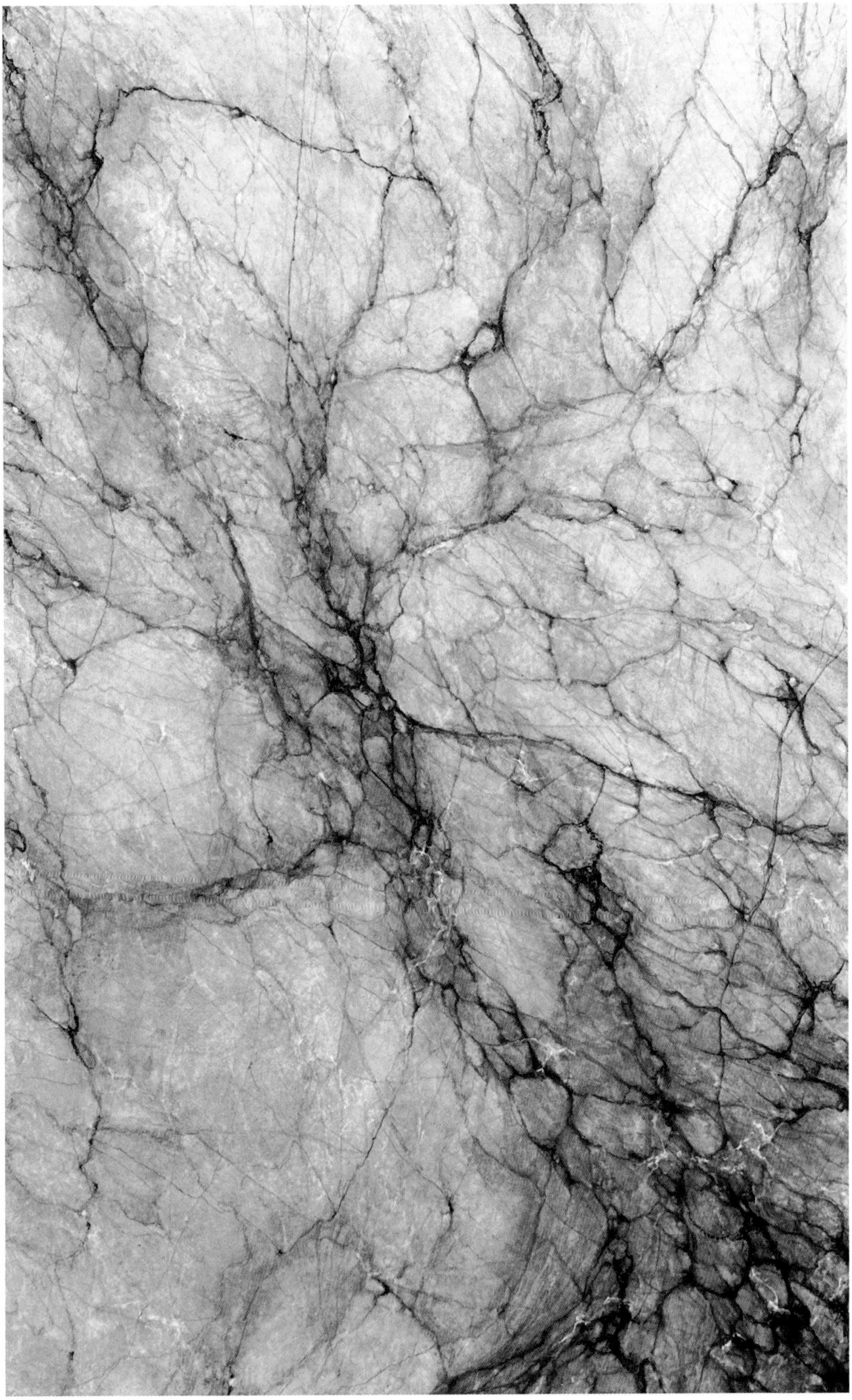

The finished piece.

Step-by-step

ANTIQUE SIENNA

MATERIALS

- oil scumble
- acrylic scumble
- artist's oil paint
  - black
  - white
  - yellow ochre
  - violet
- artist's acrylic paint
  - black
  - white
  - yellow ochre
  - burnt umber
- fuller's earth powder
- badger softener
- splayed paintbrush
- white spirit
- calligraphy brush
- cotton rag
- fine rigger brush
- round fitch
- fan fitch
- swan feather

On a white eggshell ground, apply a scumble mix of yellow ochre. Stipple with a cheap, splayed synthetic 1-inch brush. As you continue to stipple, pick up some white from your tray, and stipple, then a little black and repeat. Mix them as you stipple, forming strong ochre, black and grey areas. Have a basic formation of the marble in mind at this stage, with the darker areas near the bottom. This gives the marble a look of natural balance. When real marble was installed, the stonemasons would put the darker areas to the bottom for balance, and it is this natural aesthetic harmony we are trying to achieve.

With a damp rag, rag roll the entire surface, breaking up and slightly blending the glaze.

Slightly dampen a swan feather with water, and aggressively pull it with your hand towards the stem, violently opening up all the vanes. Then pick up some black scumble from your tray and begin veining the surface. Hold the feather from the middle and *push* it across the surface as you go, going *against* the natural fold of the feather; this will further open up the vanes and distribute abstract veining effects. Also, vary the pressure as you apply. It is this technique that gives the multi stratiform veining characteristic to many veined marbles. Repeat with white scumble, mix with black to produce grey, and apply.

With a cut-down synthetic brush dipped in white spirit, ciss the surface, and immediately blot with a clean rag.

Soften with a badger softener, lightly breaking up with the rag as you go.

With some light grey, dark grey and black, emphasise and bring together some of the vein structure, adding formation and some detail with the feather. This is done in reverse of the last technique, by using the point of the feather and dragging it softly *with* the folds of the vane. Holding the feather higher up gives you greater control in applying the detail at this point. Allow to dry.

Switch to acrylic paint, and degrease with fuller's earth. Mix a glaze of yellow ochre and stipple onto the entire surface. Rag roll with a rag and soften. Wipe out some areas to create stone effects.

continued on the following page...

With a medium calligraphy brush, apply detail with a glaze of light grey. This should be used at the outer edges of the panel only. Form stones, veining and interconnect various areas. The composition and colouring of the marble is crucial here. Lighter areas are given detail with light colour, and darker areas with darker colour.

Continue towards the centre, progressively getting darker and bolder as you go. Allow to dry.

Apply a toning glaze. This tones down the whole work, reduces the vividity, softens and takes much of the harsher veining into the background. When Marbling, the goal should be to produce great depth of colour, shape and formation. These toning layers do that. Mix a light glaze of ochre and white, and coat the surface. Rag roll and soften all. Allow to dry. Then, with a strong black glaze, bring out some of the darker veining on the panel. Allow to dry.

Apply a further toning glaze. Mix a stronger yellow ochre glaze with some white, coat the panel, and soften. Remove some areas with a rag to accentuate the breccia formations.

Now add detail. I always finish my marbled panels with fine detail veining. This can be as frugal or elaborate as you chose. I find Chinese calligraphy brushes are best for this. They are broad at the top and reduce to an extremely fine point. Used with dexterity, this can give multiform thicknesses of veins with just a slight increase or decrease in pressure. I start on the outer, lighter areas of the panel, working in towards the darker bottom area. It is important to use light glazes on the lighter parts, and use progressively darker glazes for the darker areas as you go.

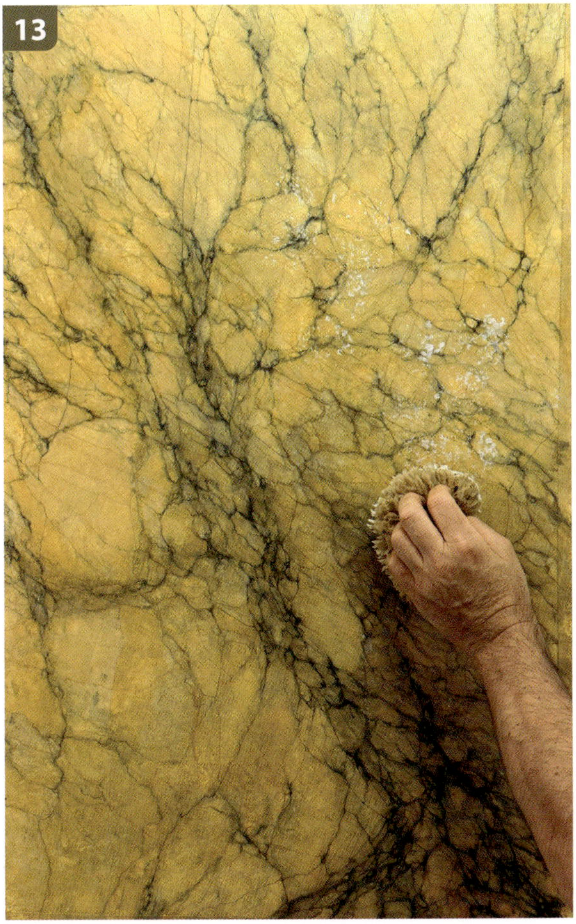

For the white detail, apply a white glaze with the pointed end of a dampened sea sponge. Break up with a rag and soften.

To finish, connect these formations with a calligraphy brush, breaking up with a rag as you go.

PART THREE ADVANCED PAINT EFFECTS

Once the painter has become familiar with the basic paint effects featured earlier in this book, he or she may want to try more advanced finishes featured in this section. Whilst historically the popularity of Graining and Marbling ensures its own category, finishes such as Trompe l'Oeil, Inlay and Gilding offer a unique chance to further your ambition and advance your newly acquired skillset.

All require thorough knowledge and experience, with Trompe l'Oeil requiring paint and glaze mixing knowledge, whilst Inlay requires experience in decorative finishes aligned with fine draughtsmanship, drawing and layout work.

Trompe l'Oeil employs intricate light and shade applications on a flat surface to create convincing optical illusions. This finish requires not only a comprehensive understanding of colour theory and perspective, but also expertise in paint and glaze mixing. Painters can skilfully manipulate light and shadow, enabling flat surfaces to appear three-dimensional. The result can transform a room or surface making it feel larger, or introduce unexpected elements such as mouldings, architraves or panelling.

Inlay is another advanced technique that involves applying materials such as precious metal, or painting marble or semi-precious stone elements onto a surface to create lavish patterns and designs. This method requires a keen eye for detail and fine draughtsmanship, as precise measuring and drawing are essential for achieving a seamless look. Inlay elevates and combines decorative finishes, making surfaces and focal points not just striking, but also works of art.

Gilding, the application of gold leaf, adds an unmatched level of luxury to any surface or design. This ancient technique creates a radiant, lustrous finish that catches light beautifully.

Exploring these advanced paint effects and techniques allows artists to push their boundaries and innovate within their own craft, resulting in transformative and visually striking skills. Mastering these techniques not only adds to the decorator's versatility, but also elevates their ability and craftsmanship to new heights.

Trompe L'Oeil exhibition panel, including painted sandstone (*see* page 22) and Antique Sienna marbling (*see* page 104).

TROMPE L'OEIL

First, what exactly is Trompe l'Oeil? Very broadly, it is the application of a semi-transparent paint glaze onto a surface to create highlights and shadows. This, if carried out correctly, will in turn give the illusion of depth and reality to that surface in the shape of forms and objects. For us, it is mostly mouldings or decorative architectural elements on a grained or marbled surface.

The actual phrase itself translates from French as 'trick the eye' and comes very roughly into two main categories: architectural (my area) and fine art. Architectural Trompe l'Oeil is usually best applied to grained, marbled or plain natural surfaces, and can sometimes be expanded to murals and large frescos. Fine art is carried out in smaller, incredibly realistic three-dimensional paintings. The artistic objective in both remains the same – to deceive the viewer into believing that what they are seeing is not a flat painted surface, but a real, three-dimensional object or scene. Ground level areas of architectural Trompe l'Oeil usually flaunt hyperrealistic detailing of mouldings, pilasters and carvings, which can trick not only the ordinary viewer, but seasoned artisans and painters alike.

The home of Trompe l'Oeil painting can be traced to ancient Greece, where the first instance was famously recorded 2,500 years ago. It revolves around the two most esteemed painters of that era, Zeuxis and Parrhasius. They proposed a competition between themselves to determine the greater artist. Zeuxis first painted grapes that were so realistic when he displayed them that a flock of birds flew down to pick at them. But Parrhasius had devised a different strategy to win. He invited

Arguably the most famous Trompe l'Oeil painting in the world, the Chatsworth Violin was painted c.1723 by Dutch artist Jan van der Vaardt. The door itself is in a passageway at Chatsworth House, Derbyshire, England. The peg has been painted on gilt metal, to enhance the illusion.

his rival into his studio to view his masterpiece. As Zeuxis attempted to draw aside the curtain to his rival's studio, he realised he had been tricked. The curtain *was* the painting, not real fabric. Zeuxis had been fooled by a Trompe l'Oeil painting so real it had deceived even his adept eye. He declared Parrhasius the winner, and famously proclaimed; 'I have deceived the birds, but Parrhasius has deceived Zeuxis'.

This encounter marked a pivotal moment in the history of Trompe l'Oeil, recording and cementing its legacy and relevance in historical decorative painting. It epitomised the very essence and magical allure of Trompe l'Oeil and is a testimony to the unparalleled power of human skill and imagination to not only approximate reality, but to convincingly replicate it.

As the centuries unfurled, Trompe l'Oeil gathered fascination and admiration. It shone through the Renaissance and spilled over into the Baroque era, capturing the imagination of the greatest minds and figures in art history. Each century brought with it its own distinctive style and unique influence, which weaved itself seamlessly into the tapestry of wall decoration to this day.

Of late, the world has witnessed a resurgence of Trompe l'Oeil painting, the intriguing illusions painted on walls and furniture a fresh and magical escape from the mundanity of mass-produced décor. Historically and today, Trompe l'Oeil has appealed to decorative artists, professional artists, and art and craft enthusiasts. The prospect of transforming an ordinary flat surface into a marble masterpiece or three-dimensional wood panelling has drawn many towards this art form. The engaging blend of illusion and reality encapsulated in Trompe l'Oeil painting beguiles many, whilst epitomising the power of human imagination and creative ideas.

Trompe l'Oeil's unique charm rests solely in its ability to fool the viewer. When you observe a Trompe l'Oeil painting so perfectly executed that it merges with reality, you do not feel any particular emotion at first: it's only when you slowly realise the three-dimensional object you are looking at is actually a flat, painted surface that it produces not only an amused bewilderment and enchantment, but an appreciation of the artistic ingenuity and skill which has been deployed.

For the effect to be successful, a Trompe l'Oeil painting must therefore have specific characteristics. It is necessary that the objects painted are represented as life-sized, respect the rules of perspective and form, and harmonise with the surrounding environment. Highlights and shadows must be credible and properly placed, and the directional light source must be considered and implemented.

For beginners, it is recommended to start with smaller, simplistic subjects and gradually take on more complex and larger-scale projects. Commitment, creativity and patience is required, and setbacks should be perceived as a chance to learn and improve, rather than as a discouragement. The results of mastering this technique are startling, and provide probably the most rewarding experience available in the whole of decorative art.

The finished piece.

Step-by-step

TROMPE L'OEIL

Trompe l'Oeil is one of the easiest of the faux techniques to learn, but one of the hardest to implement. The actual technique is simplicity itself. A piece of masking tape is applied. Then a glaze is applied and pushed towards the tape with a mottler, then softened inwards towards the tape. The tape is removed, and that's it! This technique gives you the fundamental effect required to create good Trompe l'Oeil, which is basically applying graduated light and shadow.

The difficulty is where *exactly* to put this effect; how much of it to put in, and how strong; how thick it should be, and how light or dark; the colour of it and, most importantly, the actual width of that effect!

There are three traditional ways to create Trompe l'Oeil – airbrush, straight edge and masking tape. Airbrush leaves an excellent finish, but requires expensive equipment, is time-consuming and is difficult to master. The straight-edge method is quite archaic. It is done with a wooden straight edge, fitches and blending brushes. Again, it is quite difficult to master, extremely time-consuming and leaves an inferior, unconvincing painterly finish.

By far the best technique is the masking tape method. It is easily mastered, extremely quick and effortless, and even on close inspection will leave a perfect, almost photographic representation of light and shade if carried out correctly.

The step-by-step example here is rendered on a medium-grey veined marble. The moulding is the same one I executed on the oak panel (*see* page 75). Please study this and other examples of Trompe l'Oeil in this book to become familiar with the shading, highlights and colour.

As a rule, I always make a life-sized sketch of the work I'm doing. This is critical as a reference guide to where the light and shade should go on the panel. I use acrylic, as it can be dried rapidly with a heat gun, allowing for multiple applications quickly. I find with this technique there is no noticeable depreciation in quality in comparison to oil. I actually use clear acrylic varnish as a medium on all my Trompe l'Oeil work, which dries extremely quickly, and allows for multiple immediate applications, allowing whole jobs to be carried out incredibly quickly from start to finish. However, this should only be tried by the very experienced, as it dries lightning quick, and is instantly non-reversible. Clear acrylic scumble glaze is the standard medium of choice, and perfect for the non-expert.

Note: Always try a small test piece on the actual panel first, to get the exact mixture ratios and colour perfect before you start. (Colour is discussed at the end of this chapter.)

MATERIALS

- acrylic scumble
- artist's acrylic paint
  - black
  - white
  - yellow ochre
  - burnt umber
- 3-inch mottler
- fitch

1 On your panel, faintly draw the exact moulding line positionings.

2 Always start with the largest shadows on the moulding. This will quickly help you to achieve visible structure. Using a precision edge masking tape, apply the masking tape along the edge of where the moulding should be.

3 With a fitch, apply a thin coat of transparent glaze along the whole area to be 'tromped'. This will help keep the glaze application from drying too quickly.

4 Mix a glaze of black and burnt umber, with a little water. Decide the size of the width that you want the shadow to be. Apply your premixed glaze along the edge of the masking tape, at that precise width.

5 Using a 3-inch mottler angled at 45 degrees to the surface, stipple the very edge of the glaze along its full length.

continued on the following page...

Step-by-step

TROMPE L'OEIL

... continued from the previous page.

With a 3-inch flat badger softener, badger from the outside of the band in *towards* the tape only. It is extremely critical to wipe the badger with a dampened rag after every swipe during this process, as failure to do so will result in the bristles picking up wet glaze and redepositing it, which risks ruining your work.

Badger horizontally across the band to blend the length uniformly, and one final time in towards the tape.

Remove the tape.

Dry with a heat gun if required. This will allow for multiple applications quickly.

Apply the vertical moulding shadow.

Apply the outside shadow, and small inner moulding shadows.

With a premixed and tested light glaze made up of white, yellow ochre, a touch of burnt umber and a little water, apply highlight to the bottom moulding.

Next, to finish, apply it to the smaller, inner mouldings.

COLOUR

I have taken the mouldings on this panel out beyond the marble and onto the white basecoat to give an idea of the colours I have used. I've also painted the two glaze mixes used in the shape of squares at the top on white to give a greater understanding. One of the integral parts of Trompe l'Oeil work is getting the colour of the glazes correct. The most common mistake people make is just applying black and white. This gives false, fake-looking work. The light and shadows you mix for trompe work should always incorporate the colours of the subject you are 'tromping'. Here, I have used burnt umber and black in the shadow glaze, and a light ochre and white in the highlight. A good way of achieving the correct colours is to look at the lightest part of your subject. *That* is your highlight colour. Now look at the darkest part. *That* is your shadow colour. A trick that I sometimes use is that if your subject is receiving natural light from the side or above, try placing an object on it to cast a shadow. Try and isolate that colour in your mind's eye, or even take a photo on your phone. Now maximise that photo so the shadow only fills your screen. *That* is your shadow colour.

To give some examples, a dark green vert de mer panel should incorporate dark greens in the trompe. Oak should have yellow ochres for the highlights and umbers for shadows. Rosewood and mahogany should have bright oranges and ochres for highlights and deep reds for shadows.

The golden rule is: highlights are never white, and shadows are never black.

INLAY

For the experienced decorative painter, combining just some of the finishes that appear in this book on a single panel can result in quite stunning inlay work. Decorative inlay work is a centuries-old artistic technique that involves insertion of contrasting precious materials into a base material to create intricate patterns, designs or images.

From furniture, tabletops and musical instruments to architectural elements in walls and flooring, Inlay work has been used to embellish and showcase the beauty of various decorative objects.

The art of Inlay requires skill, patience and a keen eye for detail resulting in stunning pieces that can showcase your mastery of faux painting craftsmanship.

REAL DECORATIVE INLAY

Over time the materials used in real Inlay work can deteriorate, warp or become dislodged, requiring delicate and meticulous restoration efforts to maintain the integrity of the piece. Numerous conservation projects have successfully utilised faux inlay work to preserve and restore historical objects and artefacts, where the original material, such as ivory or tortoiseshell, is prohibited or protected.

Museums, historic homes and cultural institutions have employed faux Inlay techniques to recreate missing or damaged inlaid designs on furniture, musical instruments and architectural features ensuring that these objects retain their original beauty and significance for future generations to appreciate.

For today's decorative painter, painting Inlay provides a wonderful opportunity to showcase the wide array of decorative painting skills and techniques you have acquired. As the painter behind the design of your work, you have the freedom to demonstrate your expertise and creativity in a visually striking and artistic manner.

Whether you are replicating the look of woodgrain, marble or other materials, each item must be carefully planned and executed to achieve a realistic imaginative finish.

The finished piece. On a Craquelure backdrop, I applied a semiprecious faux green onyx finish on the facets, with the four semiovals done in a mixture of variegated blue and red leaf, with a red tortoiseshell gold leaf inlay.

Step-by-step

INLAY

MATERIALS

- acrylic varnish
- gold leaf
- fan fitch

1

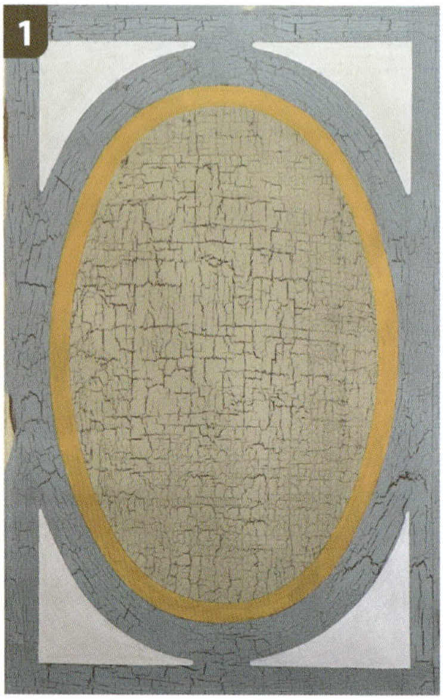

Plan and lay out your design, and apply a craquelure effect (*see* page 36).

2

Apply tortoiseshell inlay effect (*see* page 30), separated by faux boxwood strips. Marble a grey veined marble on the corner insets, similar to Carrara (*see* page 91). For the middle centrepiece, I have chosen a dark red and black background. Mask off, apply neat red and black acrylic, stipple and soften with a badger softener. Allow to dry.

3

Apply a coat of acrylic varnish.

Whilst it is still wet, immediately cover with imitation gold leaf.

Coat the gold leaf with the varnish.

Immediately manipulate and break up the leaf with a soft fan fitch, creating gaps and natural cracks in the gold leaf.

Then, before it dries, with the back of the fan brush, create veining.

Mask off areas in the shape of facets, and basecoat with white eggshell acrylic paint.

Conservation and Protection of the Earth's Natural Resources through Faux Painting and the Decorative Arts

The Earth's natural resources and species including ivory, tortoiseshell, rare marbles and precious woods are facing unprecedented threats due to human activities. Over-exploitation, habitat destruction and climate change have put these valuable materials and species at risk of depletion and extinction.

In this chapter I hope to raise awareness of the detrimental impact of humans on these resources, explore the important role of faux painting techniques in their protection, and discuss strategies to mitigate threats while preserving their beauty and cultural significance.

HUMAN IMPACT

Throughout history, man's relentless pursuit of luxury, status and profit has driven the exploitation and degradation of earth's precious natural resources.

For example, the demand for tortoiseshell, ivory, and rhino horn products has led to the decline and endangerment of these populations, pushing many species to the brink of extinction.

Illegal logging and unsustainable harvesting practices have decimated many wood species, including Cocobolo rosewood and Honduras mahogany, threatening not only the wood species, but also the local biodiversity and ecological balance of these vital ecosystems. Additionally, the quarrying of rare marbles such as Italian Sienna and Brèche Violet have resulted in landscape degradation and pollution, the loss of natural geological formations, and indeed the very extinction of the marble itself.

CHALLENGES

Addressing the conservation challenges facing these precious materials requires a multifaceted approach that combines regulatory measures, sustainable practices, community engagement and innovative, modern solutions.

Faux painting and the decorative arts offer a creative means to emulate the beauty of these resources without resorting to their unsustainable extraction.

By promoting and adopting faux painting techniques such as Graining, Marbling and unique reproductive paint effects, artists and craftspeople can raise awareness about the value of the materials and advocate for their responsible use.

SPECIES PROTECTION

To combat the illegal trade of products such as rare tortoiseshell and ivory, and help protect these endangered species, artists can utilise faux painting methods to replicate the appearance of these materials in their decorative schemes and projects.

The problems facing ivory and rhino horn have been well documented, but the dangers faced by the critically endangered hawksbill sea turtle less so. By incorporating the faux tortoiseshell featured here in this book into their creations, decorative artists can help reduce the demand for real tortoiseshell products and help promote the conservation of this beautiful marine creature and its habitat.

WOOD AND MARBLE CONSERVATION

The preservation of rare marble such as Antique Sienna and Brèche Violet can be achieved through the adoption of Marbling techniques in architecture, building and design. By recreating the distinctive colours and patterns of these marbles on alternative surfaces, the painter can minimise the need for quarrying, while showcasing the beauty and historical significance of these geological treasures.

The sustainable use and protection of endangered wood species such as rosewood and mahogany can be promoted through Graining techniques that mimic the appearance of these valuable woods by applying paint effects that replicate the rich colours and grain patterns of the world's most beautiful, but endangered, wood species. Decorative painters can raise awareness about the importance of responsible forestry practices and encourage the preservation of these precious tree species.

IMPACT AND HERITAGE

Man's negative impact on the Earth's natural resources underscores the urgent need for conservation and sustainable management strategies by integrating faux painting and the decorative arts into conservation efforts. We can emulate the beauty of tortoiseshell, rare marbles and precious woods while mitigating the detrimental effects

Illegal rosewood stockpiles in Madagascar. Rosewood and mahogany are now teetering on the brink of extinction as relentless deforestation ravages their ancient habitats. (Photo: Wikimedia Commons)

of human activities on these materials. Through creativity, innovation and a shared commitment to environmental stewardship, we can safeguard these invaluable resources for future generations, and ensure a harmonious coexistence between human development and the preservation of the Earth's natural heritage. It is through our collective efforts that we can strive towards a more sustainable and balanced relationship with the planet and its precious resources.

PUBLIC ENGAGEMENT

The importance of community engagement and education is essential to the success of conservation efforts, as is the engagement and education of communities. Educating the public about the environmental ramifications of their choices can lead to a collective shift towards more sustainable consumption. Decorative art can play a significant role in this educational mission.

Exhibitions, workshops and public art installations highlighting faux techniques can serve as powerful platforms for spreading awareness. By demonstrating how the appearance of the most sought-after natural resources on earth can be replicated artistically, with thought, training and technique, we can cultivate a greater appreciation for sustainable alternatives.

GOVERNMENT

The roles of policy and legislation play a big part in conservation. Artistic endeavours alone cannot solve the problem. Robust policy frameworks and stringent legislation are crucial in curbing illegal exploitation and promoting sustainable practices. Governments and international bodies must work collaboratively to impose bans on the illegal trade of materials such as tortoiseshell and rosewood, and enforce sustainable forestry laws. Government incentives should be provided for adopting and promoting faux painting techniques in college and training facilities. Similar incentives should be available for commercial application, making sustainable choices economically viable for businesses and production companies.

MODERN TECHNOLOGY

Advances in technology also promise new avenues for conservation. Digital imaging, 3-D printing and advanced materials science have made it possible to reproduce the texture, colour and patterns of natural resources with unprecedented accuracy. These technologies, when integrated with traditional painting techniques, can produce even more convincing faux finishes, particularly for film and TV set design. The fusion of traditional paint techniques with modern technology can redefine aesthetic standards in the modern world and make sustainable, painted alternatives more appealing.

ECONOMIC AND ENVIRONMENTAL BENEFITS

The economic benefits of promoting faux techniques are manifold. For artisans, the demand for such skills can open new markets and job opportunities. For consumers, the availability of cost-effective, sustainable alternatives can provide access to the aesthetic qualities of luxury materials without the ethical environmental downsides. Additionally, preserving natural resources ensures that they remain available for future generations, maintaining their potential economic value over the long term.

CONCLUSION

The conservation and protection of Earth's precious natural resources demands a collaborative and multifaceted approach. Painting and the decorative arts have a unique role to play in this endeavour, offering both a practical solution for reducing unsustainable resource extraction and a powerful medium for raising awareness. By education, teaching and promoting faux techniques and harnessing the power of faux art, we can emulate the beauty of tortoiseshell, rare marbles and precious woods while preserving and protecting their natural counterparts.

A future where the destructive impact of human activity is mitigated through creative and thoughtful means is within our reach. Through the combined efforts of the decorative artist, policymakers, communities and technological innovators, we can simultaneously safeguard and celebrate these invaluable resources, ensuring that they can continue to captivate and inspire us both now, and for future generations. We can embrace this challenge with creativity, determination and a deep sense of responsibility towards our planet and its irreplaceable beauty.

BIBLIOGRAPHY

1827 – Whittock, N., *The Decorative Painters and Glaziers Guide* (26 hand col plates) (Isaac Taylor Hinton, London)

1830 – (first published) *Manuel de Peintures* (Articles and Col Plates)

1841 – Mullingar Higgins, W., *The House Painter, or, Decorators Companion* (30 hand painted plates) (Thomas Kelly, 1841)

1842 – Moxon, C., *The Grainer's Guide* (22 plates, 16 hand painted) (Edinburgh, 1842)

1863 – Sutherland W., *A Handbook of Graining and Signwriting* (text only) (Manchester, 1863)

1875 – Davidson, Ellis A., *A Practical Manual of House-Painting, Graining, Marbling and Sign-Writing* (Crosby, Lockwood and Son, London)

1885 – Van der Burg, A.R. & Van der Burg, P., *School of Painting for the Imitation of Woods and Marbles* (Crosby, Lockwood and Son, London)

1891 – Wall, W., *Practical Graining* (47 col plates) (House Painting and Decorating Co., Philadelphia, USA, 1891)

1892 – Sutherland, W., *The Art of Graining and Imitating Woods,* (20 col plates) (Decorative Art Journals Co., Manchester, 1892)

1901 – Savage, W., *Graining & Marbling* (Austin Rogers & Co., London)

1902 – Hasluck, P., *Practical Graining and Marbling* (Illustrated) (Cassell & Co., 1902)

1905 – Petrie, J., *The Practical Arts of Graining and Marbling* (40 col & 4 b&w plates) (Trade Papers Publishing Co., London, 1905)

1905 – Wall, W., *Graining: Ancient and Modern* (F.J. Drake & Co., Chicago)

1941 – Burnhill, J., *The Imitation of Woods and Marbles* (Sutherland Publishing Co., Manchester, 1941)

1949 – Parry, J., *Graining and Marbling* (Crosby Lockwood 1949)

1950s – Hobbs, E.W., *Graining and Marbling: A complete Guide for Everybody* (W. Foulsham)

1953 – Derrett, J., *Graining and Painting* (Evans Brothers Ltd)

1986 – Oldenbruch, E., *Graining and Marbling / Holz-und Marmormalerei* (Edition 'Libri rari' im Verlag Th. Schafer, Hannover, Germany, 1986)

1996 – Guegan, Y., *Handbook of Painted Decoration* (W.W. Norton & Co., 1996)

1997 – Finkelstein, P., *The Art of Faux* (Watson Guptill Publications, New York, 1997)

1998 – Gray, D., *The Genuine Article*

2006 – Fleming, J., & Taylor, T., *The Life and Times of Ernest Dobson 122 Masterclasses* (Fleming Taylor 2006)

2008 – Nadaï, M., *Art and Techniques of Decorative Painting* (Éditions Vial, 2008)

2009 – Lefumat, P., *L'Art du Faux Marbres* (Éditions Vial, 2009)

2009 – Van der Kelen, D., *Decorative Painting the Van Der Kelen Way* (Éditions Vial 2009)

2011 – Laheyne, P., *The Power of Illusion* (Diligentia)

SCHOOLS OF PAINTING

Van Der Burg, A & P: Rotterdam, Holland
Logelain, Pierre: (the school Dobson attended in Brussels, which merged with the Van Der Kellen institute in the 1930s)
Van Der Kellen, Alfred: (the best known of all the European Schools and is still open today)
Schmid Engweiler: Zurich, Switzerland
Kerckhof, Leopold: Liege, Belgium (also offer courses by correspondence)
Oldenbruch, Robert: Bayern, Germany
Oldenbruch, Ernst: Vienna, Austria
Zimmermann, Wilhelm: Germany
Blott, Eugene: Reims, France
Tessier: Tours, France

The schools above taught all aspects of painting and decorating and also produced books and pamphlets on Graining and Marbling. Most of these were step-by-step guides that showed their own particular methods and techniques for the imitation of woods and marbles.

INDEX

First published in 2025 by
The Crowood Press Ltd
Ramsbury, Marlborough
Wiltshire SN8 2HR

enquiries@crowood.com
www.crowood.com

British Library Cataloguing-in-Publication Data
A catalogue record for this book is available from the British Library.

ISBN 978 0 7198 4494 2

For product safety-related questions, contact:
productsafety@crowood.com

All photography by Stewart McDonald, unless stated otherwise
Cover design by Sergey Tsvetkov
Graphic design and typesetting by Peggy & Co. Design
Printed and bound In India by Parksons Graphics Pvt. Ltd.